Collection of Articles
ON
Modern Sanskrit

VOLUME 1

RITA CHATTOPADHYAY

INDIA • SINGAPORE • MALAYSIA

ISBN 979-8-89475-314-0

RITA CHATTOPADHYAY

Contents

A Few Words

Professor Rita Chattopadhyay, a luminary in modern Sanskrit, is also my mother. She is no more amongst us and left us on 12th August 2022, that marked the mortal end of a dedicated and honest academic journey spanning more than forty years. However her rich and varied oeuvre of research contributions remains and will forever be cherished by students and scholars alike.

I don't know Sanskrit, so personally I would not be able to critically analyse her research, yet I am an academic, and from what I gather from all the books and papers which she had written (most of which are in English and Bengali which I can read and follow) and interactions with many of her colleagues and students, the depth and expanse of her knowledge and erudition in her field of research, is quite unquestionable. Not only is she remembered amongst her colleagues and students as a towering academic, her loving, caring and selflessly kind personality has touched and remain forever ingrained in the hearts of all those she had come in contact with.

I could write all her academic achievements (which have appeared on the back cover of her books and with which readers in the world of Sanskrit scholarship are familiar with, and about which I will talk a little bit in the second half of this piece), but let me take the liberty of first writing about things which may not have appeared in print anywhere and therefore less well known amongst followers and admirers of ma's works. And it is hard to capture a lifetime in a few words, so let me start by writing about an endeavour that ma undertook just a few months before she physically had to leave us.

Just before ma turned seriously ill in the summer of 2022 and from which she never recovered, she had conceptualised the birth of an organisation that we named "Convergence". Well, it symbolised the convergence of several of her dreams and visions. It started out to be an academic-cultural-philanthropic organisation, but as she herself said on several occasions, it was mostly philanthropic in all its endeavours, be they academic or cultural. Since the basic meaning of philanthropy is the desire to promote the welfare of mankind, and that is what she aimed at through all the activities and services of Convergence, ma really thought of Convergence to be a philanthropic endeavour manifesting itself in various fields like academia and culture.

One of the main motivations behind conceptualising Convergence was that she literally wanted to it be a confluence of all religions, caste and creed. At the beginning, to help with her administrative works of Convergence, she wanted to hire some students/research scholars who are not so well to do and are in need of a job – and in the hiring process she ensured that people from all backgrounds could apply. She finally hired a few of them and remunerated them amply entirely from her own savings and pension.

One of the major incentives of ma was to arrange and catalogue, and if possible, start a reference library, with the thousands of books that she had acquired over her substantially long academic life. So some of the people she hired to work for Convergence were engaged in categorising the books. Unfortunately, in the few months that she had after she started this Organisation, the cataloguing of the entire collection could not be complete, so ma actually didn't see the functioning of the Convergence Library. It is now however functioning as she envisioned – it is open for reference work that benefits many PhD scholars and researchers, that come from far and wide to avail of the access to rare books and manuscripts that ma had.

Many of her students (in her Sanskrit classes that she taught over the many years), who often came from remote areas of West Bengal, and sometimes were even first generation learners, would tell ma that they were very hesitant to go to conferences etc., because they couldn't communicate in any language other than Bengali. In fact, they were reluctant to even venture out of the state of West Bengal. It would greatly enhance their confidence and self-esteem if they could speak in English, but English language courses were far too expensive for them to afford, and also possibly not feasible given their commute. Hence one of the first things ma wanted Convergence to start with is online language courses like English.

Many of her colleagues and well-wishers in academic circles came forward and volunteered to help out with other language courses as well, and so Convergence started having these online language courses in English, German, Oriya, and Sanskrit, where the instructors and students were geographically scattered far and wide, and they could do online courses in the convenience of their homes, often late in the evening which would be infeasible for physical classes. Often students were working persons with jobs who wanted to improve their English or other language skills, or needed it for improvement in their work – so they wanted to take these courses that took place in the evenings after they returned from work.

When ma started these courses, it was free for the students and she gave remuneration to the instructors who had volunteered to teach in these courses. She herself took keen interest in many of the language courses like German and Oriya and would sit in these courses in-person. However, instructors who dedicatedly taught the courses, started to complain that services that are totally free, lose the importance and participants are sometimes irregular and lack in seriousness – hence a very small amount (that would be really a pittance in today's standards) were charged.

Among other academic activities, she also started a lecture series where people were invited to speak in their areas of expertise. And since my father's subject was Physics and mine is Economics, she always perceived Convergence to be a platform where all kinds of disciplines and knowledge converged. So we have had lectures on black holes by a physicist, on economics by an economist, on the dominance of English in India by a language expert, on the distortion of history in today's age by a historian and so on.

Among other philanthropic activities, she felicitated several senior citizens whose contributions to society have been silent and who have spent all their lives behind the limelight of public recognition, like the mother of a doctor, or the mother of a very prominent scholar, or the first teacher in a very remote rural village etc. Ma also organised sit-and-draw contests for children in such remote villages.

On the cultural front, she was a music lover and herself a trained Rabindra Sangeet singer during her youth. So she arranged for music lessons and also yoga classes under the banner of Convergence. She also started online poetry classes. ntinuing.

Given the expanse of her vision and the efforts it required, people often asked her, how does she get so much energy? What is the source of her inspiration? She often said that one of the sources of her inspiration was her work, and she went on to explain that she has composed several monographs of great Sanskrit scholars of yore. For example, she would talk of Mahamahopadhyay Haridasa Siddhanta Vagisa (on whose life she has a monograph published by Sahitya Akademi in the Makers of Indian Literature series) who single-handedly translated the original Sanskrit Mahabharata into Bengali, along with a detailed annotated version called Bharata Kaumudi.

It took Haridasa 21 years of single-handed effort and perseverance to do it. And during that considerably long time, he went through several ups and downs in life, like the loss of one of his sons. That particular evening too, he sat down with his Mahabharata translation, when another of his sons came to ask him whether he has to do it, to which Haridasa replied that 'one cannot stop at small waves coming at you when one has ventured to cross the ocean.' No wonder having worked on him as part of her PhD dissertation, she was deeply influenced by Haridasa's stoicism and perseverance, not to mention his profound erudition and prolific contribution.

Ma also spoke of other *pandits* like Gurunath Vidyanidhi, Sitanath Acharya, Srijiva Nyayatirtha, Chandrakanta Tarkalankar, Kalipada Tarkacharya, Gangadhara Kaviraja and many others on whom she has monographs, each a stalwart in their field. Gangadhara Kaviraja was so deft a physician, that the British doctors used to come to him to seek knowledge and advice during his days. She especially fondly recalled her personal interaction with Professor G. B. Palsule, who had been the Director of the famous Bhandarkar Oriental Research Institute, and a profound scholar.

Once, as a young scholar, when ma was attending a Conference in Vienna, Austria (her first international conference), she had sprained her ankle and the doctor there had given a prescription in German which she couldn't read. Having met Prof Palsule at the airport she asked him whether he could help her understand and he said he could because he knew 'a little bit of German language'. Later on ma discovered, that he had several translations of German books to Sanskrit and was an expert in German. Such humility on his part left a deep impression on ma and she recalled it throughout her life as a source of inspiration and humility.

Another personality that greatly influenced ma was Roma Chaudhuri (on whom she also has a monograph) whom she had known personally too. The stellar personality that Roma Chaudhuri was, she, along with her equally illustrious husband, Jyotindra Bimal Chaudhuri, had started an organisation called *Prachyavani* that undertook publication, had self-help groups for women, organised activities for dissemination of Sanskrit, had a library, had a wing for performing dramas etc. But unfortunately, after both Roma Chaudhuri and her husband had passed away, the organisation gradually fell apart and ceased to exist. Ma's visualisation of Convergence no doubt was greatly influenced by *Prachyavani* of Roma Chaudhuri, and she was also very concerned about what will become of it after she is no more. I am grateful to all those who are helping me take ma's vision forward and letting Convergence flourish.

Her untiring energy even at that age (she was about to turn seventy when she started this) was remarkable – she single-handedly dealt with all the calls, arranged meetings, organised events, etc – and I think ma was a true disciple and best suited to carry forward the legacy of her hero, Haridasa Siddhanta Vagisa.

She was in fact very reticent about the fact that all the expenses she incurred for the activities of Convergence and for the people working at the library etc, was borne entirely by her, from her savings, her pension and my fathers's pension. Convergence is like my sibling (I am the only child) – it is like a parting gift ma has given me to look after and bring up. Just like she nurtured it with all her love and attention, I will try to.

This book is the collection of articles of such a person – who had dedicated her life to the cause of knowledge and academia, had relentlessly pursued the well-being of the students and researchers, was unwaveringly committed to bringing into limelight scholars who have passed into oblivion, had untiringly tried to make knowledge accessible to the lesser privileged ones, and had recognised and championed the efforts and contributions of those that remain silent and relegate to the background behind the achievers. It is hard to overstate the value and contributions of such a person to society.

Let me now turn to her academic achievements, the exhaustive list of which would be formidable and hence just a brief snapshot is being presented here. She is the author of twenty eight books (including one on a collection of lesser known stories from the Mahabharata which is in Bengali and which is mainly for non-Sanskrit knowing youth) and has published several papers and made numerous presentations, both at home and abroad including University of California, Berkeley, Harvard

University, Rutgers University, New Jersey, University of Pennsylvania, USA, EHESS, Paris, Sorbonne University, Paris, France, Silpakorn University, Bangkok, Thailand, University of Vienna, Austria. Her research domain include Modern Sanskrit Literature, Epics and Puranas, Sanskrit Poetics and Dramaturgy, and Crime against women in ancient India.

As briefly mentioned before, in a significant achievement, ma had been a contributor to the Makers of Indian Literature series of Sahitya Akademi. She was the author of the monograph on "Haridas Siddhantavagisa" (2021). She had been the recipient of several awards and honours including the prestigious Emeritus Fellowship of UGC (2017 – 2019) and Griffith Memorial Prize by the University of Calcutta in 1983. She had also received a research grant from POSCO TJ Foundation, Korea for her research on "Ayurveda" (doing us Indians proud, being the only successful applicant from India). She was awarded the prestigious CIIL fellowship of Govt. of India for 1997-1998, and was nominated Chair Professor by ICCR for Paris, Bali and Bangkok (which she had to decline however).

Some of her books like "Modern Sanskrit Dramas or Bengal: 20th century AD" (1992), "Modern Sanskrit Plays" (1999), and "Modern Sanskrit Literature: Some Observations" (2004), deserve special mention for their unprecedented contribution towards bringing the then emerging stream of 'Modern Sanskrit' to limelight. Some of the other research topics close to her heart were crime against women in ancient India, aspects of the medical service in ancient India, Sanskrit and the Muslims, and Sanskrit Poetics.

Ma had truly been an academic ambassador of modern Sanskrit to the broader world around. She would often begin her talks on a lighter vein saying that to most laymen the terms "modern" and "Sanskrit" sound contradictory to each other (like *shonar pathorbati* in Bengali which means a stone bowl made of gold). Which essentially means that Sanskrit is perceived to be a dead language, and nothing modern is being depicted or composed in Sanskrit anymore. And then she would go on to claim and explain why that is a myth and the truth is that Sanskrit is still very much alive and vibrant and a lot of modern compositions in Sanskrit are based on very contemporary issues like pollution and dowry, and hence should be given very close and prime attention.

This short collection is the first attempt to bring together some of her writings that were published in various journals over her long academic career. I do hope we will be able to bring out many more such volumes covering all her deep and erudite research, that lie scattered in various journals and rough drafts for presentations.

This collection includes 9 of my mother's articles – 6 in English, 2 in Bengali, and 1 in Devanagari script. Her forte of research was modern Sanskrit, especially modern Sanskrit plays. Some some of her articles in this volume focus on these (including the articles that is written in Devanagari). But she explored various other fields as well. One of her articles in this collection also deals with how Banabhatta's Harshacaritam is a source of medical science in ancient India.

It's very hard writing a few words for a book that's ma's – she usually put in so much hard work and efforts in her books, that it's an audacity to try to match that, and I am not attempting it. Especially during the publication her later books, when her eyesight was failing due to prolonged diabetes, she had a hard time, looking at proofs, and urged the publisher to give them in larger fonts so she could go through them – she would use a magnifying glass and sit under a very bright table lamp or in the sunlight to be able to go through them.

When the newly published books would arrive, she would lovingly hold them and turn them in her hands like she was holding a baby. Her books – her labours of love, for knowledge and its pursuits, were sometimes recognised and publicly acknowledged, but more often than not, she spent sleepless nights and long hours writing them for the sheer joy of having expressed her thoughts and recording her painstaking research and findings.

She didn't care whether she received the attention, acclaim and acknowledgement commensurate to her monumental contributions to modern Sanskrit, and selflessly dedicated her life to the unconditional and unwavering pursuit of knowledge. As I mentioned earlier in the first part of the introduction, many of her books are actually monographs on the lives of lesser known Sanskrit litterateurs of India who have passed into oblivion with passing time. Hence, the very nature of her work, bringing unknown scholars into limelight, speaks volumes about her personality – selflessness and dedication, without any expectation of favour or rewards.

It's hard for me to write about ma without getting into personal reminiscences, yet I shall desist from doing so. I hope this book proves very valuable as a reference and guide for all those who are not only students of Sanskrit, but also those who are generally interested in Sanskrit, since most of the articles are written in English and hence are accessible to a wider audience.

Hope this collection lives upto the expectations she would have had from the volume. And since her birthday is upcoming, I hope she accepts this volume as a present from me. Be at peace ma, wherever you are.

Soumyanetra (Bibul)
soumyanetra.convergence@gmail.com
Kolkata
26th June 2024

P.S: Anybody who is reading this and would venture upon reading her articles, or is generally interested in getting associated with Convergence, you may please visit our website https://convergenceofthoughts.org/ and/or email me at the address mentioned above, explaining your requirements and thoughts, and I will definitely try to get back to you.

সংস্কৃত সারস্বত জগতের এক অবিস্মরণীয় নাম ঋতা চট্টোপাধ্যায়

– ড. সুজিত মাইতি
(অ্যাকাডেমিক্ অ্যাসিস্টেন্ট, কনভারজেন্স)

Full many a gem of purest ray serene.
The dark unfathom'd caves of ocean bear
Full many a flower is born blushed unseen
And waste its sweetness on the desert air.
– Thomas Gray

(অনুবাদ)
গভীর সমুদ্রে কত মণি-রত্নই তো
শোভা পেতে থাকে লোকচক্ষুর অন্তরালে।
বনস্থলে অজানা কত ফুলই তো
গন্ধ বিতরণ করে ঝরে যায় চক্ষুর আড়ালে ।।

ভুলে যাওয়া আমাদের বিশেষতঃ বাঙালীর স্বভাব। এই গভীর সত্যকে উপলব্ধি করেছিলেন যেমন ইংরেজ কবি ও দার্শনিক থোমাস্ গ্রে ঠিক তেমনই অধ্যাপিকা চট্টোপাধ্যায়ও। তাই তাঁর পছন্দের ইংরেজ কবি দার্শনিক গ্রে-র অতিপ্রাসঙ্গিক উক্তি দিয়েই শুরু করছি এই গ্রন্থের মুখবন্ধটি।

আধুনিক সংস্কৃত সাহিত্যের চর্চাক্ষেত্রে ঋতা চট্টোপাধ্যায় এক অবিস্মরণীয় নাম। পরিচিতদের কাছে তিনি সর্বদা অত্যন্ত প্রিয় ছিলেন। ছাত্র-ছাত্রীদের নিকটে তিনি মায়ের মত স্নেহময়ী। এই বঙ্গীয় বিদুষীর গোটা জীবনটা সারস্বত সমাজের সেবায় নিয়োজিত। যখনই বঙ্গে আধুনিক সংস্কৃত সাহিত্যের চর্চা হবে তখনই সহৃদয়গণ তাঁর নাম কৃতজ্ঞচিত্তে স্মরণ করবে। এমনকি আজকের বাংলায় আধুনিক সংস্কৃত

সাহিত্যকে আশ্রয় করে যে সমস্ত কাজ লক্ষ্য করা যায়, সেখানে কোন না কোনভাবে ঋতা চট্টোপাধ্যায়ের অবদান অবশ্যই বিদ্যমান। আধুনিক সংস্কৃত সাহিত্যের পাঠকদের কাছে তাঁর কাজ রত্নতুল্য। এমনকি এটাও বলতে পারি যে বঙ্গে আধুনিক সংস্কৃত সাহিত্যকে তিনিই সর্বপ্রথম চর্চার স্তরে নিয়ে এসেছিলেন। অর্থাৎ তিনি হলেন আধুনিক সংস্কৃত সাহিত্যের চর্চার আকাশে উজ্জ্বল নক্ষত্র স্বরূপ।

অধ্যাপিকা ঋতা চট্টোপাধ্যায় ১৯৫২ খ্রীষ্টাব্দে ১৯শে জুলাই কলিকাতার হাতিবাগান নামক স্থানে আভিজাত্য পরিবারে জন্মগ্রহণ করেন। ছোটবেলা থেকেই তিনি অত্যন্ত মেধাবী ছিলেন। বিদ্যালয়ের শিক্ষা থেকে স্নাতকোত্তর পর্যন্ত প্রতিবারেই তিনি প্রথম শ্রেণীতে উত্তীর্ণ হতেন। উচ্চশিক্ষা গ্রহণ কালে তিনি জাতীয় স্কলারশিপ্ পান। ১৯৭৩ খ্রীষ্টাব্দে তিনি কলিকাতা বিশ্ববিদ্যালয় থেকে সংস্কৃত বিষয়কে আশ্রয় করে স্নাতকোত্তর উপাধি লাভ করেন। ১৯৮৩ খ্রীষ্টাব্দে এই কলিকাতা বিশ্ববিদ্যালয় থেকেই তিনি পিএইচ্. ডি ডিগ্রি অর্জন করেন। সেই বছরেই তিনি সেখান থেকে গ্রিফিথ পুরস্কারের জন্য মনোনীত হন।

অধ্যাপিকা ঋতা চট্টোপাধ্যায় কর্মজীবনের সূচনা করেন কোলকাতা উইমেনস্ কলেজে (১৯৮০-১৯৯৫) অধ্যাপনাবৃত্তির দ্বারা। তারপর রবীন্দ্রভারতী বিশ্ববিদ্যালয়ে সাত বছর (১৯৯৫-২০০২) ধরে অধ্যাপনা কর্মে নিযুক্ত হয়েছিলেন। শেষে যাদবপুর বিশ্ববিদ্যালয়ে (২০০২-২০১৩) অধ্যাপনা ব্রতীর মধ্যে দিয়ে তাঁর কর্মজীবন শেষ করেন। ২০১৭ সালে এই বিদুষীকে ইউজিসি প্রতিষ্ঠান এমেরিটাস্ ফেলো রূপে নির্বাচিত করেন। এমনকি আয়ুর্বেদশাস্ত্রের গবেষণার জন্য কোরিয়ার পঞ্চো-সংস্থা তাকে গবেষণার অনুদান দিয়ে সম্মানিত করেন। ভারত সরকারের মানবসম্পদ উন্নয়ন মন্ত্রণালয় দ্বারাও তিনি সম্মানিত হয়েছেন। শুধুমাত্র দেশে নয়, বিদেশেও তাঁর খ্যাতি বিশেষভাবে লক্ষ্যণীয়। তিনি ছিলেন সুবক্তা। তাঁর বাচনভঙ্গী সহজেই শ্রোতাদের আকৃষ্ট করত। ব্যাঙ্কক, বালি, প্যারিস, ভিয়েনা, রোম, বুদাপেষ্ট প্রভৃতি দেশের বিভিন্ন বিশ্ববিদ্যালয়ে বা শোধসংস্থানে তিনি প্রায়শই বক্তারূপে আমন্ত্রিত হয়েছেন। তাই বলা হয় – বিদ্বান্ সর্বত্র পূজিত হন।

এই বঙ্গ বিদুষীর প্রকাশিত গবেষণাপত্রের সংখ্যা প্রায় ৮০ টি এবং প্রকাশিত গ্রন্থের সংখ্যা ২৮ টি। মূলতঃ এই গ্রন্থে তাঁর প্রকাশিত গবেষণাপত্র থেকে বাছাই করা ৯টি গবেষণা প্রবন্ধ নিবন্ধন করা হল। অর্থাৎ অধ্যাপিকা চট্টোপাধ্যায়ের ৯টি গবেষণপত্র এই গ্রন্থ দ্বারা পুনরায় প্রকাশ করা হল। যেগুলি আধুনিক সংস্কৃত সাহিত্যের গবেষকদের কাছে একটি মূল্যবান সম্পদ হয়ে উঠবে। তাঁর গবেষণাকাজের মাধ্যমে তিনি সদা জীবিত থাকবেন। তাই বলতে পারি – কীর্তির্যস্য স জীবতি।

प्रातःस्मरणीया ऋताचट्टोपाध्यायमहोदया

~ ड. सुजित-माइतिः

कियन्ति रत्नानि लसन्ति सिन्धोरन्तर्जले लोकदृगन्तराले।
कियन्ति पुष्पाणि वितीर्य्य गन्धं अहो विनश्यन्ति वनस्थलेषु॥

– श्रीजीवन्यायतीर्थेन

आधुनिकसंस्कृतसाहित्यस्य चर्चाक्षेत्रेषु अविस्मरणीयं नाम ऋता-चट्टोपाध्यायः। परिचितानां निकटे सा अत्यन्तं प्रियतमा आसीत्। छात्राणां निकटे सा मातृवत् स्नेहमयी आसीत्। आजीवनं सारस्वतसमाजस्य सेवां कुर्वाणा वङ्गीया विदुषी। यावत् वङ्गेषु आधुनिकसंस्कृतसाहित्यस्य चर्चा भवेत् तावत् सहृदयः तस्या नाम कार्तज्ञचित्तेन स्मरेत्। किञ्च वङ्गेषु अद्यत्वे आधुनिकसंस्कृतसाहित्यमाश्रित्य यावन्ति कार्याणि परिलक्ष्यन्ते तेषां होत्री आसीत् इयं महोदया। आधुनिकसंस्कृतसाहित्यस्य पाठकानां समीपे तत्कृतानि कार्याणि रत्नमिव परिपाल्यन्ते। यतोहि वङ्गेषु आधुनिकसंस्कृतसाहित्यं तया एव सर्वप्रथमं चर्चामार्गे आनीतम्। अतएव वङ्गेषु आधुनिकसंस्कृतसाहित्यस्य चर्चाकाशे सा तारकमिव भाति।

कलिकातायाः हातिवागाननामके स्थाने अभिजातपरिवारे १९५२ क्रैस्ताब्दे जुलाईमासे ऊनविंशतिदिनाङ्के ऋता-चट्टोपाध्यायः जनिं लेभे। बाल्यात् एव सा बुद्धिमती आसीत्। विद्यालयस्य शिक्षायाः आरभ्य स्नातकोत्तरशिक्षां यावत् सा प्रतिवारं प्रथमश्रेण्याम् उत्तीर्णा अभूत्। उच्चशिक्षायां सा जातीयशिक्षावृत्तिमपि प्राप्तवती। १९७३ क्रैस्ताब्दे सा कलिकाताविश्वविद्यालयात् संस्कृतविषयमाश्रित्य स्नातकोत्तरोपाधिं लब्धवती। तत एव सा १९८३ क्रैस्ताब्दे विद्याविरिधि (Ph.D) इति उपाधिना भूषिता। तस्मिन्नैव वर्षे कलिकाताविश्वविद्यालयः तस्यै ग्रिफिथवृत्तिम् अददात्।

ऋता-चट्टोपाध्यायमहोदया कर्मजीवनस्य सूचनां उइमेनस्-कलेज-क्यालकाटा (१९८०-१९९५) इति प्रतिष्ठानात् कृतवती। ततः रवीन्द्रभारतीविश्वविद्यालये (१९९५-२००२) सप्तवर्षं यावत् अध्यापनाकर्मणि निरता आसीत्। तदनन्तरं यादवपुरविश्वविद्यालये २००२ क्रैस्ताब्दतः २०१७ क्रैस्ताब्दं यावत् अध्यापनं कृत्वा कर्मजीवनस्य समापनं कृतवती। २०१७ क्रैस्ताब्दे विश्वविद्यालयानुदानायोगेन एमेरिटासफेलोरूपेण सा निर्वाचिता अभवत्। एवञ्च आयुर्वेदशास्त्रस्य गेवषणायै सा कोरियादेशस्य Posco-संस्थाद्वारा गवेषणानुदानेन सम्मानिता अभवत्। किञ्च इयं विदुषी भारतसर्वकारस्य मानवसम्पदोन्नयनमन्त्रकेनापि सम्मानिता जाता। एतस्याः महोदयायाः ख्यातिः देशात् वहिः वैदेशिकक्षेत्रेषु अपि परिलक्ष्यते। व्याङ्कक-

बालि-प्यारिस-भियेना-रोम-वुदापेष्ट-उइस्कन्सिन्-हार्भाड-पेनसिलभेनिया-क्यालिफोर्णिया-राटगार्स्प्रभृतीनां देशानां विविधविश्वविद्यालयेषु विविधशोधकेन्द्रेषु वक्त्रीरूपेण सा प्रायशः आमन्त्रिता अभवत्। तथाहि उच्यते – विद्वान् सर्वत्र पूज्यते इति।

तस्याः प्रकाशितगवेषणापत्राणां संख्या प्रायशः अशीतिः किञ्च प्रकाशितग्रन्थानां संख्या अष्टाविंशतिः सन्ति। मुख्यतः अस्मिन् ग्रन्थे तस्याः प्रकाशितगवेषणपत्रेषु चितानां नवसंख्यकानां शोधप्रबन्धानां यथायथं विवरणं प्रस्तूयते। गवेषणापत्रेषु चितानां नवानां प्रकाशनम् अनेन ग्रन्थद्वारा क्रियते। येन आधुनिकसंस्कृतस्य चर्चाक्षेत्रे तस्याः विचरणं सहृदयानां सकाशे स्पष्टीभविष्यतीति आशा।

20th Century Sanskrit Dramas of India: Tradition & Innovation

The primary objective of the present paper is to bring into limelight the status of Sanskrit Dramas produced in India in the later half of the 20th Century A.D.

In the short span of this paper it has not been possible to give an analytical picture of the dramas, but an earnest attempt has been made to furnish at least some introductory notes, some special features thereon.

It is true that the position of Sanskrit in modern society is degraded to a large extent; its penetration to the intellectual circle is limited and there is no commercial prospect since it is not a common lingua-franca amongst the masses. Moreover in this modern century Indian society has been subjected to a drastic change in almost all spheres of existence; the old world concepts of values are no longer honoured; the modern 'elites' find no utility of age-old Sanskrit. On the whole the scenario is totally hostile to propagation and appreciation of this rich, noble and divine language. Still there is a number of devoted Sanskrit lovers who even now in the twentieth century A.D. are trying their level best to sail against the tide and are endeavouring to make us understand that Sanskrit language can still be a force to reckon with. Some such Sanskrit-scholars and Sanskrit-lovers as well are introduced here through their works.

Since the number of Sanskrit Dramas produced under the said period is appreciably large, (i.e. more than 640) the present authoress is compelled to keep aside a good many number of outstanding works outside the purview of her discussion for which she begs to be apologized by the learned scholars. The main intention here is to focus the perfect juxtaposition of tradition and innovation in the dramas concerned and to bring the so-long-hidden talents into limelight.

Post-Independence Sanskrit Dramas have been classified into seven categories. In each category 10 dramas have been introduced and at least one drama, by way of specimen, has been chosen to justify the theme of the paper i.e. perfect juxtaposition of tradition and innovation. In the process an attempt is made to touch upon some provinces of this vast peninsula-India. Of course, with a focus on Bengal.

I. HISTORICAL PLAYS:

In this category, more than sixty historical plays produced in this century have been traced some of which are based on the ancient period of Indian history e.g. on Candragupta, Asoka and so on; some historical dramas are based on medieval Indian history; some on the history of modern period e.g. on freedom movement of India, on Kashmir problem under the administration of Nehru and some on some important event of world history e.g. on the birth of a new nation Bangladesh. Some of the historical plays are enumerated below.

BĀNGLĀDEŚODAYAM – by Ramkrishna Sharma of Uttarpradesh 1972,

Delhi 1988, 2nd ed.

The present drama with 10 acts is a faithful portrayal of historical events and historical characters e.g., Yahya Khan-the Pakistani General; Zulfikar Ali Bhutto-the Pakistani political leader, Sheikh Mujibur Rahaman-Bangladeshi political leader, leader of Awami league in East Pakistan (later Bangladesh).

Here the dramatist seems to be in his best in the last śloka which would be considered as Bharatavākya where Mujib wishes deep friendship between India and Bangladesh and expresses hope for communal harmony between the Hindu and the Muslim.

Gangā Yamunā yāvad Vangasindhuhimālayau/Vaṅgabhāratayor maitrī tāvat sthāsyati bhūtale /

svādhinā smo vayantvadya svaśramaphalabhoginaḥ/Gītā-Qurānayoḥ pāṭham kuryāsmaḥ sahitā sada //

INDIRĀVIJAYA: (Andhra Pradesh, 1972)-by Venkataratna. This is a one – act-play divided into a number of scenes, mainly based on the political strategy adopted by Smt. Indira Gandhi, the former Prime-Minister of India, during the Bangladesh movement.

KĀMGRESA-PARĀBHAVAM: (Reva Prasad Dwivedi, Madhya Pradesh. 1977) (Defeat of the Congress) This is a drama in 10 Acts. Indira Gandhi's appeal to the Supreme Court against the Judicial verdict of Allahabad High Court, the defeat of Congress party led by Mrs. Gandhi and the victory of Janata dal and Morarji Deshai as well in 1977 election are wonderfully delineated.

SVĀTANTRYA-YAJÑĀHUTI: (Dr. Narayan Shastri, Samskrita Ratnākara (J), 1956, Jaipur, Rajasthan), on freedom movement held at 1942.

APŪRVA-ŚĀNTI-SAṂGRĀMAḤ: (Viswanath Keshab Chatre, Viśva – Saṃskṛtam (J)1972, Bombay), on Satyagraha movement made by Gandhiji.

SATYĀGRAHODAYAḤ: (Ramlinga Shastri, Composed in 1969, on the occasion of Gandhi birth-centenary, Hyderabad, Osmania University,) on Satyagraha movement initiated by Mahatma Gandhi.

BHĀRATA-LAKṢMĪNĀṬAKAM of Dr. Jatindra Bimal Chauhduri on Lakshmi Bai, the queen of Jhansi.

SUBHĀṢAVIJAYAM (Mans) Pt Nityānanda Smṛtitīrtha, Bengal. This drama deals with the political career and stormy life of Subhas Chandra Bose popularly and widely known as Netaji and deals mainly with his prolonged fight with the British for the freedom of India.

AMARAVĪRAVṚTTĀNTAM (Mans) Pt Nityānanda Smṛtitīrtha, Bengal. This

drama deals primarily with the execution of Khudiram Bose, a patriot of 18 years only.

VĀLEŚVARA-MAHĀYUDDHAM: (Mans) It is a drama in five acts written by Pt. Nityānanda Smṛtitīrtha of Bengal. This drama deals with the patriotic activities of Jatindranath Mukherjee (8.12.1879 – 10.9.1915) widely known as Bagha Jatin of Bengal and especially with the Baleswar fight where sacred martyrdom of Bagha Jatin was gloriously held.

In almost all the 10 dramas mentioned above the commendable blend of Tradition and Innovation is distinctly found. We would like to comment upon the last mentioned one Vāleśvara Mahāyuddham.

Yatindranath, the here of our play, with his all the qualities e.g. indomitable courage, zeal, mental strengh is vividly portrayed in V.M.

yatīndranātho bhuvi suprasiddho /
netā sadaiṣām bahusāhasī hi/
vaṅgaprasūto bahulokanetā /
karoti ceṣṭām mahati sadaiva // (V. M.-sl 26/p.12)

That this political *sannyasi* had the personality of a dedicated soldier is evident from a number of references of our text. Revolution was the mantra of this sannyasi who wanted India's emancipation in two stages-political freedom and social and political change (V.M. p.5, P.15, p15, p.23 etc.)

Besides, the inhumane tyranny of the British officials e.g. Tegard and so on, (VM. p. 11/sl 20., p16/sl 37) the patriotic zeal of the followers of Yatindra have graphically been portrayed by our playwright.

V.M. a fine book which with simple style and diction not only testifies to the author's deep grounding in Sanskrit language but also his fine literary talent.

The death of hero, though a notable and remarkable departure from convention, yet the success of the play lies in the message of the primary import of laying down Yatindra's life unhesitatingly to free his motherland from the shackle of imperialism. Though it is mentioned in the dramaturgical text vadho yuddham caibhir varjitah etc. SD/VI, still innovation is found in representation of the hero's death new dimention has been given, a novel perspective can easily be traced.

II. BIOGRAPHICAL PLAYS:

Biographical literature is an important and significant sector of Modern Sanskrit Literature.

Internationally significant religious and spiritual figures like Sankaracharya, Ramakrishna, Vivekananda; political personalities like Mahatma Gandhi, Pandit Nehru, Lokamanya Tilak, Rajendra Prasad, Churchill, Dr. Bidhan Ch. Roy, Indira Gandhi; popular saints and mystics e.g., Jnanesvara, Ramdasa, Tukaram and well known scholars like Max Muller, Rabindranath Tagore have become the subject of biographical dramas.

Actually, writing Biographical dramas on historical personalities, is undoubtedly a very difficult task. Biographical work should not be a mere history or biography, i.e. an insipid statement of dates and facts nor can it be a mere 'fiction' or 'fantasy' soaring only on the wings of imagination however, sweet or charming. Thus an author of biographical poetry – be it either in poetic or in dramatic form – has to steer between two extremes; history and imagination, cautiously but artistically. Thus the proper and perfect synthesis of history and literary art; truth and fiction lies at the root of the success of a Biographical Play. In this category also more than (60) sixty dramas have already been traced. To name a few : –

BHĀSKARODAYAM: This is a novel biographical drama of mahānāṭaka type, in 15 acts, based on the early life (upto 25th year) of poet Rabindranath Tagore, written by Dr. Jatindra Bimal Chaudhuri, of Bengal published by Prācyavāṇi, Calcutta in 1961.

The language of this drama is a unique one and captures the hearts of the connoisseurs. The language is simple yet dignified: true to the point yet sweet; modern, yet following the traditional rules. Some portions of speeches, poems and songs of Rabindranath, have been wonderfully and successfully rendered into Sanskrit, retaining to a large extent, the cadence, spirit and sublimity of the original.

i) Bha – Act XIV /

> divāloko nirvāti bhāskaro'stagamī/
> nabhaḥkroḍe megharāśiścandramadhukāmī//170
> meghopari megha āste varṇo varṇopari
> mandire kamsyaghaṇṭā dhvananamādhurī//171
> pāre dūre vṛṣṭipāto luptaṃ tarukulam/
> pāre'smin meghabhāle maṇijivaladalam// 172
> varṣāmeghe smarasi nu śaiśava-saṃgītam
> saśabda, patati vṛṣṭiḥ sroto vanyāsphītam//173

ii) cf, Original Bengali –

> diner ālo nibe elo. suyyi ḍobe ḍobe /
> ākās ghire megh kareche cāder lobhe lobhe/
> megher upar megh kareche – raṅera upar raṅ,
> mandirete kāsar ghaṇṭā vājla ṭhaṅ ṭhaṅ/
> o parete vṛṣṭi elo jhapsa gachpala/
> e pārete megher māthāy ekso māṇik jvālā /
> bādlā hāoyay mane pade chelevelār gān –
> vṛṣṭi pade tāpur tupur, nadey elā vān /

Saṃkalitā by R.N. Tagore, Calcutta, 1996.

iii) In English-

> The Rains fall pattering down
> The light of the day is fading
> The sun is setting soon
> The clouds gather in skies
> Desirous of the moon. (Trans. of sl 170).
> The rain-winds bring to mind
> A song of childhood great :
> The rains fall pattering down
> The rivers are on spate. (Trans. of sl. 173).

Rabindranath, the first Indian to win the coveted 'Nobel Prize' for his nonpareil creation – Gitanjali – a book of spiritual lyrics – is by common consent the greatest poet of Modern India, and, also, universally honoured as a 'Viśva-Kavi' – or a world-Poet. He is, as yet, unsurpassed, if, both the quality and the quantity of contributions be taken into account. He is honoured in India and abroad, not only as a great poet and litterateur, but also as a great educationist, social reformer, patriot, philosopher, religious teacher, humanist, music-composer and musician, painter, artist, orator and what not! Writing drama on such a renowned and significant personality is no doubt a very difficult task, But, in Jatindra Bimal's 'Bhāskarodayam', a perfect juxtaposition of history and literary art; or facts and fiction – is found. Our author most surprisingly but successfully has steered clear of both the extremes and composed a unique drama – which is based on facts, yet is a drama in the truest sense of the term, – with original situations, beautiful descriptions, interesting dialogues, lovely poems and exhilarating songs. With all these and with his other biographical plays of appreciable merit. Dr. Chaudhuri claims a unique and unshakable position – not only as a first rate dramatist but as a great biographer too – in the history of Modern Sanskrit Literature.

Last but not the least, Dr. Jatindra Bimal's drama emits the fragrance of a deep spiritual fervour – so refreshing in this modern age of cynicism.

TUKĀRĀMA-CARITAM: (Originally written in form of poetry by Kshama Rao in 1950, later on dramatized by Lila Rao.) a one-act play dealing with the life and spiritual activities of the great poet, saint and devotee, 'Tukarama', (app. 1608-49 A.D.) of Maharashtra.

LOKAMĀNYA-SMṚTIḤ: (S.B. Velankar, Maharashtra) two-act play based on the patriotic activities of the famous Indian nationalist leader Bal Gangadhar Tilak.

DHANYO'HAM-DHANYO'HAM: Written by Dr. G. B. Palsule of Maharashtra. A play with 4 acts, (where the Acts are further subdivided into scenes) is based on the life of Vinayak Damodar Savarkar, popularly called Veer (Valiant) Savarkar (1883-1966), the grand personality who was a hero of India's fight for freedom from the British thraldom.

MAXMULARA-VAIDUSYAM: by Bhavani Shankar Trivedi, 1981, is a drama on the scholastic activities of the great Sanskrit scholar Maxmuller of Germany.

KEŚARĪ CAṂKRAMA: Shibaprasad Bharadwaj, Viśva-Saṃskṛtam, (J) 1963, Hosiarpur, Punjab, on Lala Lajpat Roy.

ĀYURĀROGYA-SOUKHYAM: E. P. Bharata Pishrodi, Eranellur Trichur, Kerala 1st Ed, 1989. The theme of the play is based on the eventful early period of the life of Melpathur Narayana Bhattapada, who according to our author, an extraordinary genius in the field of Sanskrit literature, especially in grammar and poetry, can hardly be compared with any poet or scholar of the later centuries.

SRĪ GĪTA-GAURĀṄGAM: Dr Birendra Kumar Bhattacharyya, Calcutta – 1974, A lyrical Play (Giti-natyam) on the life and religion of Gaurāṅga Caitanya, the great preacher of selfless love towards both man and god.

SIDDHĀRTHACARITAM: Dr Birendra Kumar Bhattacharyya, Calcutta, 1970. A drama, in 8 Acts, based on the life and positivistic

Philosophy of Gautama Buddha, the great proponent of the doctrine of non-violence.

In case of Biographical plays too synthesis is found. But a few words have been put forward regarding Bhasakarodayam of Bengal and Vivekanandavijayam of Maharashtra.

VIVEKĀNANDA-VIJAYAM: (S. B. Varnekar, pubd. by Vivekānanda Rock Memorial committee, Madras; 1972, Maharashtra)

This is a homage to Vivekananda, by the author, in the the form of a drama. In this drama (a mahānātaka in 10 Acts) – a perfect synthesis of history and imagination is traceable. Exercising his imagination the playwright brings out the spirit of the life mission of the hero, – the Hindu Sannyāsi Vivekānanda of International renown. Prof. Varnekar's poetic mind seems to be influenced to a great extent by Ramakrishna Vivekānanda movement.

So far as the technique and structure are concerned the drama is very much conventional since the type is of mahanataka with 10 Acts, *Nāndī*, *Bharata-Vākaya* are very much present. But innovation is found in absence of any Rasa as such.

We would like to place the beautiful translation of Vivekānanda's Chicago Addresses, at the World's Parliament of Religions held on 11th September, 1893 (in its first session) in the spacious hall of the Art Institute.

It is now a well-known fact that no sooner had he addressed the assembly of more than 4000 people – men and women representing the best culture of the United States as 'Sisters and Brothers of America' than a great wave of enthusiasm went through the audience. They rose to their feet with shouts of applause, as if they had gone mad. Everyone was cheering, cheering and cheering. The Swami was bewildered.

Our author seems to be quite competent in expressing Vivekananda's appeal-

"amerikiyā   bhaginyo!   bhrātaraśca!........sarvadharma-sahiṣṇutā sarvamatasamādaraśca viśvasmai jagate yena sadaiva pṣṭhitaḥ, tasmin hindudharmiye samāje jāto'ham iti mahān mama abhimānaviṣayaḥ..... rūcinām vaicitryādṛjykuṭila nānāpathajusam nṛṇāmeko gamyastvasi payasāmarṇava iva".

"I am proud to belong to a religion which has taught the world both tolerance and universal acceptance. We believe not only in universal toleration, but we accept all religions as true. I am proud to belong to a nation which has sheltered the persecuted and the refugees of all religions and all nations of the earth.

As the different streams having their sources in different places all mingle their water in the sea, so, O Lord the different paths which men take through different tendencies, various though they appear, 'crooked or straight, all lead to Thee".

III. PLAYS BASED ON MODERN TOPICS:

This category appears to be most important of all.

What is worth mentioning and which is inspiring at the same time is that the Sanskrit-scholars, like any other scholars in any field are also affected by the turmoils and vicissitudes of the pressing problems of the society.

Verily, some sections of the Sanskrit scholars of present century still cling to the old, time-honoured theory of literary exercise, they cannot accommodate any deviation from their conservative outlook. But the exceptions are a large number of 20th Century Sanskrit playwrights, short story writers and novelists. 20th Century Sanskrit scholars like all other social beings of the present century are also affected by the pressing problems of the society. The trend of selecting themes from contemporary political social, academic, industrial scenes and treatment thereof, either in serious veins or with sarcasm, is evident in their writings, Problems of modern India, socio-economic, political, psychological or so didn't lie beyond the range of the visions of Sanskrit litterateurs who normally are known for their bigotry and for clinging to the time-honoured theme, theory and technique. Thus, people, generally considered to be aloof from all the vicissitudes of socio-political tangles, too cannot but respond to society's call.

Thus the dramas on 'Indo-China war', Kashmir issue, on 'widow marriage', on 'child marriage', on ' Superstition' e.g., child-immolation, on 'Refugee influx', on Demoralization of society', 'System of Democracy' System of Bureaucracy', India's quest for unity, Torture on and humiliation of womanfolk', communalism, 'Apartheid' and on many more issues in the context of present social milieu deserve mention.

CAṆḌA-TĀṆḌAVAM – is a serio-comic playlet representing the horrors of second world-war in a sarcastic way written by Pt Śrījīva Nyāyatīrtha of Bengal.

VEṢṬANA-VYĀYOGAH – is a playlet on *Gherāo* written by Dr. B. K. Bhattacharyya of Bengal published at Calcutta in 1971 A.D. There cannot be a stronger satire on the policy of *Gherāo*. V.V. is characterized by fresh approach, novel thought and by 'modernity' – in true sense of the term.

DHARITRĪ-PATI-NIRVĀCANAM (Calcutta, 1971) – is an enjoyable satirical playlet, based on the contemporary political condition of the whole world, written by Dr. Siddheswar Chattopadhyay of Bengal. There cannot be any stronger attack or any pointed satire on contemporary political condition in international scenario. The International body known as UNO (United Nations Organization); the super powers with their huge arsenal of deadly weapons; the policy of non-alignment of neutral nations with their unjustified pride and many more aspects of contemporary political scene get lashes of sharp satire from the facile pen of our author.

ATHA-KIM – Atha Kim is a Sanskrit playlet of satirical type (*vyaṅga nātikā*) written by Dr. Siddheswar Chattopadhyay of Bengal (popularly known as Burodā) in 1969.

Atha Kim is a savoury Sanskrit playlet with a severe reproof towards our system of Democracy, towards all the political parties of Bengal rather India and especially towards our polling system at the time of 'Election'.

Herein, no story as such is found. All the characters are introduced by mere symbols and not by individual names; since, in each case the personal identity of the individual is not important, important is the 'class' or 'the political idea' they represent. Thus all the characters, representative of different classes etc., are introduced, interestingly enough, with a peculiar combination of vowels and consonants e.g. Kaḥ Khaḥ etc.

NĀNĀ-VITĀḌANAM (S.S.P (J), Calcutta, vol LVII, 1974) – This is a savoury Sanskrit play of satirical type written by Dr. Siddheswar Chattopadhyay of Bengal, based on the present humiliating condition of Sanskrit.

There cannot be any sharper satire on those 'elites' who being at the helm of academic affairs shed crocodile tears for the abolition of Sanskrit but inwardly endeavour for her abolition from all the academic curiculas in West Bengal.

MĀTṚHANANAM & JANANĪSRĀDDHAVASARAM – two playlets by Nityananda of Bengal; SAMSKṚTAVĀGVIJAYAḤ by Prabhudatta Shastri of Delhi are on the same theme of present condition of Sanskrit.

JANANĪ – Janani is a modern one-act play by Dr. Gauri Dharmapal of Bengal (pen-name Uma Devīsūrya) written in September 1984. The work is not yet published.

'Janani', with its lucid style, simple but dignified language, with occasional use of Bengali language, with its novel theme revealing the identity of 'Mother' – of the 'House Mother', of 'Sanskrit', of India' and of 'mother soil' or Earth', bringing out the multi-lingual and the integrated aspect of India, depicting integration in its different aspects e.g., family integration, linguistic integration, national and East-West integration and with an ultimate objecive of ushering into the traditional realm of peace, harmony, tolerance and integration– will ever be enshrined in the hearts of the connoisseur.

TRNAJĀTAKAM – (1983, 1st ed, Himachal pradesh) – This is anone-act play divided into a number of scenes written by Pandit Durgadatta Shastri of the Kangra district in Himachal Pradesh.

The drama shows how the usurer amasses wealth by taking advantage of the impoverished people who are generally subjected to extortion. It exposes the harmful system of Bonded Labour (p-16) and highlights the restrictions connected with the caste-system etc. In a nutshell, the drama pointing out some darkest corners of our socio-economic system in the present century deserves appreciation from all.

YAUTAKAM – (Varanasi, 1986 A.D.) – Yautakam is an one act play written by Shivaji Upadhyay of Uttar Pradesh. The play shows how the harmful system of 'dowry' still now prevalent in our modern society is oppressing the father who is burdened with a marriageable daughter for whom marriage can't be settled without a huge amount of dowry for the bridegroom.

The style is lucid, language is simple and topic is modern and relevant to this present day society. Our author says sarcastically-*Yautakam nanu sarvasvam yautakam mānamūlakam, yautakam kanyakā śūlam, yautakam varamūlyakam.*

and draws our attention to this problem of our society.

Abhiṣṭamupāyam (1986, U. P) by Abhiraj Rajendra Miśra; *Pariṇītā* (1983, Pune) by Ogeti Pariksit Sarma, *Somaprabhavam* (in the press) by Radhaballabh Tripathi of M.P. are other excellent dramas on the same theme of dowry and brideburning.

DARIDRADURDAIVAM (Calcutta, 1968) – by Srijiva Nayatirtha of Bengal on demoralization of present day society.

HAKĪKATARĀYANĀṬAKAM – by Hazarilal Sharma of Haryana on Communalism.

In all the above mentioned Dramas Innovation' plays a major role compared to traditon. For that rcason, all the mentioned dramas have been encompassed as representative ones.

The plays based on contemporary political issue e.g. on Kashmir problem or on U.N.O. which throw some sarcastic fling are also included in this catgory .

IV. PLAYS BASED ON THE EPISODES OF UPANISADS / PURĀNAS / RĀMĀYANA / MAHĀBHĀRATA:

Form time immemorial Rāmāyaṇa, Mahābhārata, Purāṇas etc. are the eternal source of continuous flow of themes and ideas that are woven into literary creations. Quite obviously the dramas based on Purāṇas etc are huge in number. More than 150 dramas are traced in this category of which a few are being intorduced.

GUPTA-PĀŚUPATAM – (Bombay, 1975) – by Viswanath Satyanarayan of Andhra Pradesh, based on the episode of Mahābhārata, gives a new interpretation of the great Kurukṣetra war.

NARTANAŚĀLĀ – (Bombay, 1983), by Ogeti Parikshit Sharma of Andhra Pradesh, based on the Kīcakavadha-episode of Mahābhārata.

ŚRAVAṆAM – by the same author is based on familiar episode of Daśaratha's life (i.e.killing of the blind sage by Dasaratha) traceable in Rāmāyaṇa.

EKACAKRAM – (Bangalore, 1990) – by N. Ranganatha Sharma of Karnataka deals with the episode of Kunti and Pañcapāṇḍava found in Mahābhārata.

ŚAURI-ŚAURYAM – by Jaggu Singaracharya deals with Kṛṣṇa's exploit in boyhood from Visnu Purāṇa and Bhāgavat Purāṇa. The playwright has remodelled the purāṇic theme with a few remarkable innovations.

MAHĪYASĪ GĀRGĪ – (Calcutta, 1976 A.D.) – by Brahmacāriṇī Belā Devī of Bengal is based on the story of Bṛhadāraṇyakopaniṣad.

NACIKETAŚCARITAM – (Calcutta, 1976 A.D.), by the same authoress of Bengal is based on the wonderful story of Naciketa found in Kaṭhopaniṣad. In all the works of Bela Devi, to restate the lofty ideas of ancient India preached by Vedas, Upaniṣads etc. seems to be the primary aim of the authoress who herself is associated with some religious institutions.

PRĀYOPAVEŚANAM – (Howrah, West Bengal, 1972 A.D.) by Pandit Durgaprasanna Vidyābhūṣa a of Bengal, is based on the episode found in the Vanaparvan of MBH. (the episode of the sage Durvāsas and his disciples).

EKALAVYA-GURUDAKṢIṆAM – (Calcutta, 1971 A.D.), by the same author is based on the tragic Ekalavya episode found in the Ādiparvan of MBH.

MĀṆAVAKAGAURAVAM – (Calcutta, 1958) by Mm. Kalipada Tarkacarya is an elegant play with seven acts based on the story of MBH about the great sage and the teacher Dhaumya and his disciples.

In all the above mentioned dramas tradition plays a major role regarding theme, but innovation is noticeably found in the reinterpretation of the themes.

Let the case of the last drama be considered. Apparently the playwright predominantly belongs to the old tradition and he follows the technique and the style of the raditional dramatists; he uses *nāndī*, *bharatavākya*, *sandhis*, etc. in a most conventional way, but the drama primarily aims at the glorification of *"gurubhakti"* i.e., the devotion to a teacher, which is an essentiality for student community, without which a student cannot achieve anything and which has attained a lean and thin body in the present-day society. A character personifying the abstract quality e.g. gurubhakti and a number of gnomic verses are inserted for the glorification of the said quality – an essentiality for the modern age.

V. PLAYS-BASED-ON-QUASI-HISTORICAL-EPISODES / LEGENDS / ANECDOTES:

A novel and appreciable trend is very much prominent among the Sanskrit dramatists of twentieth century A.D. to reconstruct the lives and personalities of the great poets and poetesses through the form of a drama. In most of the cases they have based their themes on the anecdotes or legends centred around the lives of some celcbrated figures e.g. Vālmīki, Kālidāsa. Sometimes the authors have created the plays from the minimum of the matter with them e.g. a few verses found in the anthologies or quoted in some other Sanskrit texts. In this category we have met near about twenty five dramas some of them are enumerated below.

BHĀSOHĀSAḤ – (Pune, 1980) – this is a non-pareil play, written by Prof. G.B. Palsule of Maharashtra, with three acts where the acts are again sub-divided into scenes.

The plot is completely imaginary but still centres round the traditional story of burning of all the dramas (except Svapnavasavadattam) of Bhasa by the judges recorded in the famous lines – *bhāsa-nāṭakacakre pichekaikṣipte parīkṣitum* etc.

Dr. Palsule, the author of this drama has successfully and strikingly enough tried to give a splendidly rational interpretation viz. that society did not tolerate that the playwright should not be faithful to the sacred writings of Vyāsa and Vālmīki; or the society would not tolerate the poet like Bhāsa (the hero of this drama) who should have made heroes out of villains. It shows further that an author if he is true to his ideals may often pass through ordeal.

ĀNĀRKALI – (Madras, 1972) – is a ten act play written by Prof. V. Raghavan of Madras, based on some well known quasi-historical romantic episode connected with the secret love between Salim (later on emperor Jahangir) and Anarkali-immaculately beautiful lady (attendant) in the mughal haremn.

The play is a great step for national integration. It projects an overall ideology of integration and harmony.

ĀDIKAVIḤ – (Bharati (J), Bihar) – by Buddhadev Pandeya of Bihar on the life of Kālidāsa.

KĀLIDĀSA-MAHOTSĀHAḤ – (staged at Ujain) – by H.C. Devekar of Madhyapradesh on the life of Kālidāsa.

KĀLIDĀSA CARITAM-(Maharashtra, 1961) – by S. B. Velankar on the life of Kālidāsa.

PREKSANAKATRAYI – by Dr. V. Raghavan of Tamil Nadu

i. VIJAYAṆKĀ
ii. VIKAṬANITAMTAMBĀ
iii. AVANTĪSUNDARĪ

on three famous poetesses of India

PREMAPĪYUṢAM – by R.B. Tripathi of Madhyapradesh on the quasi-historical incidents connected with the life of the poet Bhavabhūti

BHARTṚHARĪYAM – by V. D. Gangal of Maharastra on the life of Bhartrhari based on the famous verse of Nītisataka *dhik tam ca tām ca.*

DASYU-RATNĀKARAM – by Viśveśvara Vidyābhuṣaṇa (Mañjūṣa (J), 1957)

ĀDIKAVERUDBHAVAM – by Jayashri Nag, Burdwan, W.B., 1984 A.D

PRAŚĀNTA RATNĀKARAM – by Mm. Kalipada Tarkacarya (S.S.P.P. (J) Calcutta, 1938-39)

All three are based more or less on the theme of how bandit Ratnakar was transformed into Vālmīki – the great poet of Rāmāyaṇa.

Thus in this category also 'tradition' plays a minor role i.e., tradition is followed regarding structure. But as regards theme and spirit innovation' is Conspicuously traceable in almost all the dramas.

VI. PLAYS ADAPTED / TRANSLATED FROM OTHER LANGUAGES:

Translations are esteemed to be as important as the creative works, since they fulfil a double purpose, viz that the works in the Sanskrit language are enriched in one hand, on the other these are helpful to understand the literary values of the original creations in other languages especially the vernacular ones and thereby contribute to national integrity.

DINĀRKARĀJAKUMĀRA-HEMALEKHAM is a Sanskrit version of William Shakespeare's **Hamlet** by Dr. Sukhamay Mukherjee, published at Delhi in 1971 A.D. The **Hamlet** has been acclaimed as the greatest among the tragedies of Shakespeare. Moreover, it is esteemed as the most popular as well as most problematical play ever written.

The original **Hamlet** is indeed noted for abundance of such quotable apophthegms. Our translator's successful renderings of such passages deserve special attention and acclaim here. The advice of Polonius' to his son Laertes, Hamlet's observations on man in Act II before Rosencrantz and Guildenstern and of course the famous and profound "To be or not to be" of Hamlet are worth mentioning here.

CANDRASENAH is another outstanding translation of **Hamlet** by S.D. Joshi & Vighnahari Deo of Pune (Maharashtra); **Yūthikā** (1976) is the translation of famous Romeo-Julliet of Shakespeare by Revaprasad Dvivedi of Madhyapradesh. Besides a number of translations are made in dramatic form from vernaculars e.g. Marathi, Telegu, Bengali. More than 20 of Tagore's dramas/short stories have been translated in the form of drama. Of which **Vālmīki-pratibhā** (New Delhi, 1966) by V.

Raghavan of Madras, **Ratharajjuh** (S.S.P (J), 43ʳᵈ yr. No. 8-12) by Dr. Bimal Krishna Matilal of Bengal; Muktadhārā & Vārtāgṛham (Calcutta, 1963) by Dr. Dhyanesh Narayan Chakravorty of Bengal; **Sampatti-samarpaṇam** (Howrah (W.B) 1987) by pandit Nityānanda Smṛtitīrtha of Bengal deserve special attention.

MUKTADHĀRĀ AND VĀRTĀGṚHAM

Muktadhārā, the greatest of Tagore's symbolical play and Dākghar – a gentle and deeply moving play have successfully and elegantly been translated by Prof. Dhyanesh Narayan Chakrabarti being titled as **Muktadhārā** and **Vārtāgṛham** respectively.

However in consideration of lucidity and simplicity, application of selected sounds these productions are indeed joy for ever to Tagore-lovers and Sanskrit-lovers as well. It seems all of them have proved the inappropriateness of the saying

"The perfume of a pristine thought / Can't in translation be caught."

By way of. specimen, mention may be made about the followving. In the first Act after the exit of the curdseller, Amal says (intoning) "Curds, Curds, Curds..., from the country of the panch-mura hills by the Shamlibank, curds, good curds, in the early morning the women make the cows stand in a row under the trees and milk them and in the evening they turn the milk into curds, curds, good curds", etc.

Where Tagore says – «*dai, dai, bhālodai, sei pāñcmuda pāhāḍer talāy samli nadir dhāre gaylāder bāḍir dai. Tārā bhorer velāi gācher talay goru dāmḍ kariye dudh doy sandhyāvelāy meyerā dai pāte sei dai*».

And Dhyaneshnarayana almost in the same tone and spirit says – (Gitasvarena) dadhi, dadhi, uttamamdadhi, tadhi pañcacūḍaśaila tale syāmalinadī tīravartighoṣagṛhānām dadhi, te hi prabhātakāle dadhi, te hi prabhatakale dadhi – da – a – dhi, uttamam dadhi etc.

Those, in the audience, who do not know Bengali, they even can note amazing and starting resemblance between the two versions – the Bengali (original) and its translation in Sanskrit.

In this category, there is no scope as such to point out the synthesis of tradition and innovation. Because a good translator has little scope to show his innovative acumen.

VII. PLAYS ON MISCELLANEOUS TOPICS:

There are a large number of dramas which are found to be difficult to place within the periphery of any particular category as such because almost each and every of them is a category by itself. So it seems to be appropriate to club all those together in this category which may be termed as 'Miscellaneous'. In this category a sharp departure from traditional track is found and naturally innovation plays a major role.

CONCLUSION:

Much more still needs to be said about *20th Century Sanskrit Dramas* of India. Through this present paper it has been tried to point out different novel trends which are distinctly traceable in the compositions of 20th Century Sanskrit playwrights. Some of them observe the traditional rules of dramaturgy to some extent and introduce certain experiments in theme, technique and spirit as well A large number of playwrights have selected the themes of their plays from contemporary social, political, academic and industrial scenes occasionally with sarcastic fling towards the society and the individual as well. In most cases modern dramatists have ventured with the ultimate optimistic objective of ushering in a better society – full of peace and harmony. Another appreciable trend most conspicuously found in modern dramas is the trend of projecting the ethical values through the well-known episodes of Upaniṣads, Rāmāyaṇa, Mahābhārata and Purāṇas. Besides, the trend to translate or to adapt from the works of great literary artists e.g. Shakespeare, Kālidāsa, Rabindranath Tagore, Bankim Chandra and many more and thereby to project the philosophy of those artists as reflected in the original – is very much prominent in the works of the dramatists of the present century and to reproduce the great lives of the great souls of India in order to inspire the present generation is another noteworthy trend found in the modern dramas.

Sometimes the themes are traditional and innovation is found in the formation of structure and application of technique: in some cases the technique is traditional and innovation is found in selection and reinterpretation of theme, and in the rest cases 'innovation' perfectly overrules 'tradition'.

There are 20th Century Sanskrit Dramas which prove conclusively the high potentiality of the language and establish positively that even modern rather ultra-modern thoughts and incidents can be easily and wonderfully expressed in Sanskrit language.

The present authoress has carefully chosen a few number of dramas produced in different parts of this vast peninsula with a special focus on Bengal to highlight the deviations and innovations mentioned above. She has made an humble attempt to establish the fact that though Sanskrit has lost its honourable status yet undoubtedly it continues to be to some extent a potential vehicle of thought and emotion. Above all, she has tried to draw the attention of the international congregation of elites towards the commendable juxtaposition of 'radition and innovation', 'tradition and modernity' which is conspicuously found in "20th Century Sanskrit Dramas' of India.

But it is a matter of great regret that good many Bengali rather Indian prodigies – in the vast domain of Modern Sanskrit Literature, with their outstanding contributions not only in drsyakavya or drama section but in other fields too, – are passing into oblivion.

As a devoted lover of Sanskrit the present researcher will consider her humble effort amply rewarded if she has been able to draw attention of the connoisseurs towards the neglected and so-long-hidden talents of Modern India.

The more she goes deep into the subject the more is her feeling of not being able to project the different facets of this treasure upto her satisfaction. She is very much aware that there is much more scope of work in this vast area of Modern Sanskrit Dramas where she has ventured to tread on.

She dares take up presentation of this because she places all reliance on the connoisseurs who may be esteemed in the following maxim (of a 20th Century poet) with a little change,

doṣākaram praṇayaphulladṛśā vilokya/

tuṣyani ye paraguṇaikaparā mahantaḥ/

sambhāvyamānabahudoṣaparī tametam

(gaveṣaṇā) patram vidhātumiha me paramāśrayāste//

[Oh! noble souls

Thou see the beauty of the Moon

Making its stains obscure,

So this little endeavour

May receive thy blesings for ever

Making me feel secure] (Tr.)

A LIST OF ABBREVIATIONS

Atha — Atha kim by Dr. Siddheswar Chattopadhyay. (Buroda). Calcutta. 1974.

Ba — Bāṃgladeśodayam by Ram Krishna Sharma, Delhi, 1988. 2nd edition.

Bh — Bhāsohāsaḥ by Dr G. B. Palsule, Pune. 1980

Bha — Bhāskarodayam by Dr. J.B. Chaudhuri, Calcutta. 1961

C.T — Caṇḍatāṇḍavam by Sri Śrījīva Nyāyatīrtha, Calcutta. undated

Dha – Dhāritrīpatinirvācanam by Dr. Siddheswar Chattopadhyay (Buroda), Calcutta. 1971

Hem – Dinārkarājakumāra-hemalekham (A Sanskrit version of William Shakespeare's Hamlet) by Dr. Sukhamoy Mukherjee, Delhi, 1971. 1st ed.

J – Journal

Mans – Manuscript

MBH – Mahābhāratarn

Mm – Mahāmahopādhyāya

P – Page Position

Pt – Pandit

S.S.P – Sanskrit Sahitya Parishat, Calcutta.

Tr. – Tṛṇajatakam, Ist ed. Durgadatha Shastri, 1993. H. P.

V.M – Vāleśvaramahāyuddham

V.V – Veṣṭanavyāyogaḥ

[*Note* – This paper was presented at the 25th Annual Conference on South Asia, University of Wisconsin, Madison, U.S.A. October, 1996. And was published in the Journal of the Department of Sanskrit, Rabindra Bharati University, Calcutta, Vol. VI, 1994 – 96.]

2

20ᵗʰ Century Sanskrit Dramas: Changes in Technique

Adaptation to modern dramatic technique in the Sanskrit plays of the last three decades is also a remarkable event in this context.

As found in western plays the acts are generally divided into scenes. Occasionally there is no act-division; the play is divided into a number of scenes. For instance, nine plays *Kā Vārtā*, *Mādhuryam* etc. published in Navamālatī (New Delhi 1997) composed by Nodanath Mishra may be mentioned. A number of other plays also may be named as the cases in point.

The essential gorgeous forms of the stages are transformed into simplified forms due to progressive outlook of the playwrights. The influence of group-theatre playes and of Marxist dramas especially of E.F. Brecht can't be denied. Sometimes the Characters acting some roles play the part of some inanimate objects. The play *Masakadhānī* (vide Saptaka – P-43), in which four persons act as four stands of a mosquito-net, may be cited as the most relevant example here.

The orthodox concept of a firm barrier between the stage and the spectators has been removed giving a new dimension to the dramatic technique. Occasionally, the characters performing on the stage are seen to come out from spectators underlining the inseparable identity between the characters performing on the stage and the characters watching as spectators. Thus in the play *Ganesapūjanam* (by Radhavallabh Tripathi, published in Saptaka), five or six persons from the first row of the audience act as the characters of the play (Saptaka – P-53).

Abstract plays, Radio-plays (Nabho-nāṭya or śruti-nāṭya), symbolic plays, operas or Gītināṭyas, street-plays are produced. One-act plays infringing the dramaturgical conventions (Pañcādika – S.D. (vi) are being produced and performed in a considerable number keeping pace with the fast life of the modern age. The introduction of 'Flashback' system in Sanskrit plays is a noticeable feature indeed, (Sapta – P-186-187). At times, all the characters, especially in the Abstract plays, are introduced by mere symbols and not by individual names since in each case the personal identity of the individual is not important; important is the class or the idea they represent. Thus, interestingly enough in Atha kim by Siddheswar Chattopadhyay of Bengal, all the characters, representative of different classes etc., are introduced with a peculiar combination of vowels, consonants and spirant (visarga). For instance, therein 'kaḥ' represents the educated middle-class people who have lost all interests in politics and can't be swayed easily by political propaganda of the political party-leaders, 'khaḥ' represents the lower middle-class people who are hard-pressed and are finding it quite difficult to meet all the basic necessities in present socio-economic and socio-political situation of India. 'gaḥ', 'ghaḥ', ' ṅaḥ' etc. represent spokesmen of different political parties of India.

In this context the plays published in 'Mṛtyu ' etc. by Dr. Harshdev Madhav may be mentioned with special emphasis. The influence of 'third theatre' as publicized by the noted director and thespian Shri Badal Sarkar of West Bengal can conspicuously be observed in Harshdev's plays. All the plays are either 'abstract' or 'symbolic' in character. The play 'Kabrasthāne', through the conversation of two spirits exposes sarcastically the hollowness of human life. In the play titled 'Kāmala' the deadly disease 'jaundice' has been depicted to symbolize all pervading decadence in present day society. In almost all his plays, the playwright shows how human beings are drifting along aimlessly everlost in the labyrinth of mundane needs and worries. All of Harshdev's plays bearing symbolic and significant titles and having high doses of histrionic clement are undoubtedly an outstanding departure from the conventional track. Though the playwright has tried to present some plays as surprising stunts, yet whether they are all that praiseworthy or not leaves work for the connoisseur.

Besides, a number of dramas of the said period do not belong to the same traditional pattern. For instance, there are modern plays in Sanskrit avhich are neither 'sutradhāra-krtārambha' nor divided into 'aṅka' etc; neither they begin with conventional 'nāndī' nor do they end with 'bharatavākya'. There is no ' nāndī' in a good many numbers of plays e.g. *Nanāvitāḍnam, Kāvārtā, Madhuryam, Raktābhisekam* etc. In some places, 'nāndīs are there, but conventional deities e.g. Viṣṇu, Śiva, and so on are not invoked. So in the play "Uttiṣṭha Kaunteya", Śrīmadbhagavadgītā has been worshipped: 'nāndī' of "Svapnājjagaraṇaṃ varam", invokes God of dream ! At places, 'nāndīs are there but in unconventional form. The nandi of the play *'Dārāskohīyam'* (Sapta-P-151) where our country, India speaks about herself roughly in the form of an autobiography may be cited as a wonderful instance.

There are plays ending without 'bharatavākyas'; morcover there are plays ending with conventional 'bharatavākyas' but in unconventional form *'Cakrānusaraṇam'* (Sapta-P-200), *'Dārāskohīyam'* (Sapta-P-2 8), *Badhū-dahanan* (Tri-P-53-54), *Dvesadamsanam* (Tri-P-81). *Veṣṭana-vyāyogaḥ. Raktābhiṣekam* (Rudra-P-117) may be mentioned as relevant pieces here.

Different songs are inserted in the plays. Each and every one has got its distinctive flavour strikngly but exclusively of its own. Most of the songs have got some unstrained and spontaneous appeal. The songs of the labourers eulogizing *Veṣṭana* or Gherao (V. V-P-5, 7), the sarcastic song in *Ja*, the 'Gazal' song in Navamālatī (P-72), the chorus song of the common people depicting decadence in democracy and exposing Bofors scam (Parṇa-P-2) and many more are extremely suitable to their respective situations. 'Kirtan' style in the song of *Nanāvitāḍnam*, '*Bhajan*' and pop song in '*Dhanam*' deserve special mention in this context.

The modern playwrights in general are found to be very much careful about the background music. They clearly indicate the specific tone of the music reflecting the mood of the situation. As such happy (prasannatā-dyotakam kṣipram-samgitam-Sapta-P-112), or melancholic (avasādasamgītam-Sapta-P-112), Light or serious (gambhira dhvani-Sapta-P-174) moods are reflected through the back-ground music. Besides different sounds e.g. the typical sound of the taking off and landing of the air-crafts, (vimānāgama dhvaniḥ, vimāna-prasthāna-dhvaniḥ, etc. Sapta-P-135,138,140), of the chanting of Vedic hymns (Sapta-P-145), twittering of the harbingers of dawn (Sapta--P-144) and many more effect-music are distinctly indicated by the playwrights to make the performance of the plays casier and more enjoyable too.

Thus we find as with the themes, so also with the dramatic technique, a perfect blend of tradition and innovation in Sanskrit playes of the last three decades.

Some noticeable traits of Modern Sankrit Language: Words, Population maxims, literary idioms.

As with the themes, so also with the literary idioms, a perfect blend of tradition and innovation in the terms of coined words, allusion, popularid maxims and the like brings forth a new mode of stylistics of figurtive language.

Prākṛt, the conventional language for ceṭī vidūṣaka etc. is omitted in almost all the plays under discussion probably to make the understanding of the general viewers easier Sometimes vernaculars e.g. Bengali. Punjabi. Oriya. and Hindi etc. are used.

Occasionally words, idioms or popular maxims from English language and Persian too arc used comfortably instead of Prakrit or vernaculars. Some examples are given below : Rūparudrīyam p-53, 54, 57 etc.)

1. E Dad! what a silly idea-p-7
2. E You shut up madam-Rudra-p-$3
3. E Oh ! my god-Rudra-p-54
4. E Oh ! I see-Padam-p-126
5. E Halo ! who is Engineer. Parna-49
6. E You are like a moon darling ! Parna-p-59
7. Persian-Sapta-p-152-1 53

Some authors have come forward to coin new words. A list furnishing a good many number of such coined words used in Modern Sanskrit Literature along with their English or vernacular counterparts is given below:

English / Vernacular	Sanskrit
Loud – speaker/	dhvaniyantra/
Hand – mike	dhvanivistārakayantra
Bar-cum-Restaurant	pānaśālā
Cup-board	kapāṭika
Bottle	bātila
boy-bearer	bālasevakaḥ
bearer who serves drinks	madhu-vyavasthāpaka / madhuvitarakah
Tables /wooden tables / tea-tables	tebulani / kāṣṭhamancāni /
Pastry	kāsṭha-pīṭha
Tea	piṣṭskam
Coffee	cā, cahā, cāy
Toffee	kafi, kāfī
Bread/ Loaf	tāfī
Morning alarm – sound	roṭikā / beroṭikā
door-bell	ghaṭikodvodhaka – dhvaniḥ
Electric-heater	dvāra-ghaṇṭikā
Shaving-brush	vaidyutoṣṇaka
Electric-calling bell	śmaśru-kurcikā
	vidyud – ghaṇṭikā-svaraḥ

L. T – starīyāḥ

'High-School' Parīksa	**'Police'** – Sthānam nayanti
'Civil-surgeon'-am	Maxiḥ,
'Desuza-Pādriṇā'	Nightgown-am

Occasionally some words or literary idioms, from vernaculars, without change or with a very negligible change have easily crept in literary language. A good many number or such words of idioms from vernaculars e.g. Bengali Oriya, Hindi, Maratlhi, Telugu are listed herewith :-**hā, didi, he-e-e-e, hā-hā-h-a, re-re-re, hum, ko ko, peyājī, gherao,dādā, lungi, mavāli, uḥuḥ, uhuhu, chiḥ chiḥ chiḥ, he he he he, lucikā, dāla, idli, dosā, upmā, pāyas, huzur, sarkār, tāk dhin tāk dhin, jhan jhan jhan, dhak dhak, dhak, chaṭ paṭ chaṭ paṭ, khaṭ khaṭ lotakāyitā** etc.

Sometimes some urdu words are Sanskritized on the basis of phonetic or semantic similarity for instance **khara-svabhāvaḥ (khara-dimāg), salam-huzur, viśarmānaḥ (beśaram), doṣajam (dojakham), prasrab (pesab), surādhi (surāhi)** etc.

Though in most of the above mentioned cases the syntactic justification is not easy to find out yet the novel venture definitely deserves appreciation.

"The popular maxims are to a language what pillars are to a building" so to understand modem Sanskrit language in its identity it is obligatory to understand the pillars thoroughly may they be from vernaculars e. g. Bengali, Marathi, Kannada, Telugu etc. from foreign languages or from Classical Sanskrit itself.

A very few such popular maxims comfortably used in modern Sanskrit Literature along with their similar counterparts traceable in other languages are being illustrated below.

1.a. prathame grāse makṣikā-pātah – Madlura-P-4, P-10
b. prathama-grāse makṣikāpātah jātaḥ – Padam-P-75
c. prathama-grāse makṣikāpātaḥ – Parṇa-35.

This popular maxim meaning 'stumbling at the first step' is common in a number of languages e.g. English, Arabic, Urdu, Persian, Bengali, Hindi etc. Some of them are being illustrated below:

(i) **English** – stumbling at the first step.

(ii) **Bengali** – pratham grāsei (pātei) māchi paḍlo.

(iii) **Hindi** – khichdi khate pahuca utra.

2. (a) kṣut – kṣāma-kaṇṭhasyodare muṣaka yātāyātaṃ kurvanti – Madhura-P-8.

(b) kākaḥ krandanti mamodare-Vivek.

The maxim, with similar idea, meaning 'someone is extremely hungry' is traceable in the vernaculars eg. Bengali, Marathi, and in Classical Sanskrit too where Vidusaka often says-

"kṣudhayā khādito'smi"

Compare-

(i) **Marathi – mājhyā potāta kāvale orakhā āheta.**

(ii) **Bengali – khidete peṭe chucoy dan mārche.**

3. (a) **Chātrināṃ pauṣamāsaḥ,**

mama tu sarvanāśa – Janani (Mans)

(b) **muṣikasya prānāpatti**

biḍālasya keli – Bhukailāśanāṭakam P-3.

meaniag 'what is sport to someone is death to someone else' is directly borrowed from the following Bengali proverb:

Bengali –

Kāro pauṣ mās kāro sarvanāś

Almost similar idea is traceable in other languages too. For instance,

(i) **Telugu (Tr)**

sport to the cat is the death to the rat.

(ii) **Kannada – bekkig cellāṭa ilige praṇasaṃkaṭa.**

(iii) **Hindi-**

koi mare koi salhar gā ve
(iv) **German (Tr)-**
what is sport to the cat is death to the mouse.
(v) **Danish (Tr)-**
What is play to the strong is death to the weak.
(4) **baddhā muṣṭi lakṣādhika – mūlya-Pādadaṇḍaḥ**

This proverb is directly borrowed from Marathi proverb as follows :-

"jhākli muth savvā lakkācī"

This has a wide application in Marathi. The proverb literally means a closed fist (jhaklimuth) (contains) a lac and a quarter (Rs.1,25,000/ – etc.). It means sometimes it is advisable to observe silence or to speak very briefly in order to conceal your ignorance or prevent disclosure of facts which should better be left unsaid.

It may be used in the context where a person tries to hide his insult from some one, to hide his poverty or in the opposite direction to hide his real income from Income-Tax Officer.

(5) **ko nāma madhuramiti ikṣudaṇḍam samulam cuṣati ca?**

– Padadanda by Banamala Bhaolkar,

The authoress has translated as it were the following Marathi proverb in Sanskrit.

Marathi-
"us goda lāglā mhanūn kā koṇi mulāpāsun khātam"

which literally means sugarcane is sweet, still you don't eat all its parts; a part from bottom is left out. Similarly, you may enjoy something but don't exploit it too much, don't take undue advantage of it.

Compare-
Telugu (Tr)-

Because the sugarcane is sweet are you to chew it with the roots?

(6) dvādaśavarsāni Rāmāyaṇaṃ śrutvā pṛcchati Sītā – rāmayoḥ kaḥ sambandhaḥ – Dhanyo'ham dhanyo'ham

meaning 'to tell a tale to one who is in a slumber' is common in the following languages.

(i) Ecclesiasticus: (Tr.)

"He that telleth a tale to a fool speaketh to one in a slumber; when he hath told his tale, he will say, what is the matter?"

(ii) Telugu (Tr.)

Like asking what relation Sita was to Rama after listening to the whole Ramayana.

(iii) Hindi

sārī rāt kahānī sunī aur subaha ko pūchā zulekhā aurat thī aur mard.

(iv) Bengali

sāt kaṇḍa Rāmāyan śune Sītā kār bāp?

(7) ākāśaṣthivanamātma-sīrṣoparyeva patati – Ruparudrīyam-P-85.

(i) Telugu (Tr)

If you spit when lying on your back it will fall on your face.

(ii) French-

Who spits against heaven, it falls on his head.

(iii) Spanish-

He who spits against heaven will have it fall on his face.

(iv) Eccle-sias-ticus – xxvii/25 sec. 27

"who so casteth a stone on high casteth it on his head".

(v) Bengali-

upare thuthu chetāle nijer māthāyi paḍe.

(8) stutitarau āropayati – Samānamastu vo manah.

-meaning literally "to make somebody climb a chana-plant" from Marathi original.

"ekhā thyālā haramamānyā jhāāvara caḍhavaṇe"

which actually means to praise somebody out of all proportion with some ulterior motive.

(9) kintvatra tu dīpasya tale' ndhakarameva – Navamālataī – P-23.

Compare:

(i) **English-**

Roguery hides under the judgement seat.

(ii) **Telugu (Tr)-**

It is alwayas dark underneath a lamp.

(iii) **Hindi-**

cirāg tale andherā.

(iv) **Bengali-**

pradīper tālatei andhakār.

Some popular maxims or literary idioms used in Modern Sanskrit dramas alongwith their corresponding sources in vernaculars are given below:

(i) **bhavatāṃ mukhe ghṛta-śarkarā** – Navamālataī / P-40.

cf. Hindi – muhame ghī śakkar

Bengali – tomār mukhe phulchandan paḍuk.

(ii) bhavantaṃ āśikha-nakhaṃ pītavastraiḥ alaṃkariṣyāmi – -do – P-40

cf. sārā aṅga sonā diye muḍe deva. (B)

(iii) riktamastiske anarthaṃ karma prasphurati eva – do – P-56.

cf. śunyamastiṣka śaytāner bāsā (B)

idle brain devil's workshop. (E)

(iv) yāvat svāsaḥ tāvat āsaḥ--do – P-56

cf. yataksan śvās tataksan ās (B)

CONCLUSION

Now, I come to the concluding part. Why the modern Sanskrit plays are not wellknown that is a separate issuse 22 languages are accepted and recognised by Sahity Akademi. Among them Sanskrit is the only language which is not spoken. Dogri even is the spoken language. Now, what is a भाषा भाष्यते इति भाषा। So shouldn't we call Sanskrit a 'भाषा' or language Should we go for 'लक्षणा here? Should we accept मुख्यार्थवाध here? Let us think over it. In a Sanskrit conversation camp, or in a कविसम्मेलन we speak absolutely in Sanskrit. Does it mean that Sanskrit is a भाषा or whatsoever? In the village of Karnataka, everybody speaks in Sanskrit, does it mean or can we expect Sanskrit to be revived by that? Absolutely not. However, that's a separate issue.

Now Academic world does not mean the world of Sanskritists only. I am clarifying dramatists or Literateurs like Girish Karnad, Mohan Rakesh, Utpal Dutta all are well-known names. But who ever outside the Sanskrit world knows G. B. Palsule, Siddheswar, Srijiva, Keshab Das, Sitanath, Dipak Ghosh-these stalwarts of 20th century Sanskrit literature?

We know नान्दीकार चेतना and so you who became famous by performing Brecht on stage. Do we know the person who brought Brecht first-not only in Bengali or Indian stage but in total South Asian stage – He is Siddheswar Chattopadhyay?

How far unknown let me clarify-

नरक गुलजार of Manoj Mitra of Bengal was staged and performed in 1977. All the newspapers applauded – "यदि वलि वांला नाटक एइ प्रथम तार आत्मशक्ति फिरे पेल ताहलेओ वोधहय सवटुकु वला हय ना। 'नरक गुलजार' तार चाइते वेशी किछु दावी करते पारे। यदि से वले 'political drama' वल्ते प्रकृतपक्षे या वोझाय, एइ प्रथम ता मञ्चस्थ हला। मने हय कारो किछु वलवार थाकवे ना।

Tragedy is, *Dharitripatinirvacanam* was staged 1969 and published in 1971. That is absolutely a political drama with point blank satire. So good many dramas in Sanskrit are composed and successfully staged much before 1971. But the academic world is totally unconcerned about the dramas composed in Sanskrit. We know Brecht, we observe Brecht centenary, we know the dramatists and group theatre people. But we do not know Siddheswar.

Thus almost all the Sanskrit literatures with all their contributions are passing into oblivion. But we, the teachers, students, researchers and lovers of Sanskrit can't deny our responsibility. I quote-

नवं नारिकेलं नवीनञ्च चेलं। रमां चापि नव्यं नूतनञ्च गृहं
वचश्चाप्यपूर्वं विशेषण सर्व्वं। रसज्ञाः पुराणाच्चिरायाद्रियन्ते ॥

"Sweet is the water of coconut when it is weed (ডাব)
sweet is the saree when it is new,
sweet is the bride newly wed
sweet is the house newly made
sweet is the lecture when it tells somethings novel.

New things are there where 'Rasikas' (connoisseurs) always revel.

[*Note* – This paper was published in *Sumedha Journal* 2008-2009 (Viswa Bharati), Page – 56]

Bāṇabhaṭṭa's Harṣacaritam: A Source of History of Medical Science in Ancient India

What is the objective of my paper is very clear through the 'abstract' which has been distributed to all of you.

It goes without saying – In order to make proper justice to the topic which I have chosen, necessarily, I have to touch upon more or less five allied areas:

1. Harsavardhana's reign
2. Bāṇabhaṭṭa
3. Bāṇabhaṭṭa's *Harṣacaritam* (hereafter HC)
4. Some aspects of Medical Science in Ancient India.
5. Some aspects of Medical Science as traced in Bāṇa's *Harṣacaritam*

I quote from History of Ancient India, by R.S. Tripathi, –

"The seventh century A.D. begins with the appearance of a remarkable figure on the political stage, and although Harsa had neither the lofty idealism of Asoka nor the military skill of Chandragupta Maurya, yet he succeeded in arresting the attention of the historians like both these rulers".

There are very few among the rulers of india whose history is so rich in both contents and materials as the history of Harṣavardhana.

To reconstruct the history of Harṣavardhana's reign the following contemporary works are worthmentioning:

1. Bāṇa's हर्षचरितम्।
2. Yuan Chwang's or Hiuen Tsang's Si-yu-ki i.e. Records of his travels.
3. A number of seals.
4. Epigraphs.

Among the last two to name the most important ones are:

1. Banskhera copper plate of Harṣavardhana.
2. Madhuvan copper plate of Harṣavardhana.
3. The Sonpat copper seal.
4. The Nālandā seals.

Which deserve mention.

In all available resources mentioned above except very little in Hiuen Tsang's description we hardly find any discussion on the prevailing medical practices until we come to Bāṇa's *Hrṣacaritam* which has depicted a detailed account especially on the practical aspect of Medical Science developed during Harṣa's reign.

Hiuen Tsang, the famous Chinese traveller was in India from 629 A.D. to 645 A.D. He has left extensive memoirs of his travels, in which he speaks in detail about a king Harṣa who was the emperor of northern India. Although there are slight discrepancies in the accounts of Harṣa furnished by Bāṇa and the chineses pilgrim, the points of agreement are so many and so striking that there is not the least doubt that the emperor Harsa, the patron of Bāṇa, is the same as the great monarch of whom the Chinese pilgrim has left extensive notices. Harṣa is said to have reigned from 606 A.D. to 648 A.D.

Therefore Bāṇa must have flourished towards the end of the 6th and in the first half of the 7th century of the Christian era.

A good deal of evidence, may be set forth, which strongly corroborates the above conclusion regarding Bāṇa's date. Ruyyaka (1150 A.D) mentions Bana; Namisādhu, the commentator on Rudrata's काव्यालङ्कार,

Bhoja, Dhananjaya and others, confirm the date. Kṣemendra, (latter half of 11 cen. A.D./1088 A.D) mentions Bāṇa. Quotations from Ruyyaka, and many other references may be mentioned in this connection.

The Harṣacaritam has the distinction of being the first attempt at writing a prose-kāvya on a historical theme. He gives a contemporary picture which is indeed important but its importance as an document of political and social history should not be overrated.

Bāṇa was the court-poet of king Harṣavardhana (606 A.D. – 647 A.D.) of the pushyabhūti dynasty of Thaneswar and Kanauj. His work, the Harṣacaritam, written about 620 A.D. is a contemporary account of deeds of Harsha during the earlier year of his reign. According to the noted historian Radha Kumud Mukherjee *"thus in Bāṇa Harṣha found his Boswell."*

The progenitor of Bāṇa's family, Vatsa, lived in a place called Prītikūta (प्रीतिकूट) on the banks of the हिरण्यवाहु, otherwise called Sona; Bāṇa's mother, Rājādevī or Rājyadevi died while he was yet a child. He was all the more dear to his father, who was a very mother to him. Bana had the misfortune to lose his father chitrabhānu when he was about fourteen years old. Bāṇa tells us that he thereafter led a wandering life.

Although Bāṇa had ancestral wealth sufficient to maintain him in ease and comfort, yet his strong curiosity to see different lands impelled him to wander from place to place and made him an object of ridicule in the eyes of elderly contemporaries. According to some, he mixed in dubious company. However Bāṇa, during his company acquired evil repute as well as a rich harvest of wisdom and experience.

Cf. अभवञ्श्चास्य सवयसः समानाः सुहृदः सहायाश्च। तथा च भ्रातरो पारशवौ etc: HC-I

Now, while defining काव्यकारण Mammata says – शक्तिर्निपुणतालोकशास्त्रकाव्यद्यवेक्षणात् etc. (Kāvyaprākaśa – I) in which Dandin's view regarding काव्यकारण has been repeated as it were.

नैसर्गिकी च प्रतिभा श्रुतं च बहुनिर्मलम्। अमन्दश्चाभियोगोऽस्याः कारणं काव्यसम्पदः॥ Kāvyādarśa – I

This combination of three elements may be traced in almost all the works of well-known litterateurs irrespective of language. The noted Bengali author Samaresh Basu (Kālkūṭ) gives a vivid details of the foot-sores of the fishermen in his novel *Gangā*. His व्युत्पत्ति is prominently exposed in his another novel अमृतकुम्भेर सन्धाने too.

Somerset Maugham (1847-1965) spent his early and middle years in England or in farranging travel abroad in search of materials for numerous books, stories, numbering well over 200 are the finest products of his inexhaustible traveller's mentality. As a traveller he wrote

"I filled notebooks with descriptions of places and persons and the stories they suggested…. I kept my eyes open for character, oddness, personality…. I learnt very quickly when a place promised me something and then I waited till I got it."

However in Harṣacaritam we find Bāṇa mentions as the companions of his wanderings a number of persons e.g.

अभवंश्चास्य वयसा समानः सुहृदः सहायाश्च। तथा च भ्रातरौ पारशवौ चन्द्रसेन-मातृषेणौ, भाषाकबिरीशानः, परं मित्रं, प्रणयिणौ रुद्रनारायणौ, विद्वांसौ वारवाण-वासवाणौ, वर्णकविः वेणीभारतः, … भिषक्पुत्रः मन्दारकः, जाङ्गुलिको मयूरकः, आक्षिकः अखण्डलः,…मस्करी ताम्रचूडः

Bāṇa's travel-companions were as diverse as from the writer to the dancing girl, from magician to musician, singer, painter, gambler, the snake-doctor; or dealer in antipoison, or antidotes; from a young physician to the manufacturer of dolls (पुस्तकृत्), from वांशिक or Flute-player to beautician (संवाहक).

So it is quite natural there will be references to a number of places, varieties of characters and a number of शास्त्रs,

However, ample references to Medical Science scattered all over Harṣacaritam are our present concern. We will come to this central point again after discussion of some other points directly or indirectly related to the central theme

Now, we would like to judge whether medical science was one of the subjects taught in ancient times or not.

According to Yuan Chwang, (Hiuen Tsang) the most distinguished centre of learning in that age was the far-famed University of Nālandā, which then counted 10, 000 students on its rolls. Even *'foreign students came there to put an end to their doubts and then become celebrated'*. Some of these came even from Mongolia. The history of this University needs special treatment, but here it is relevant only to notice such facts and conditions as are connected with the time of Harṣa and with the medical science as well. The subjects of study at Nālandā, were not confined to Buddhism alone. Though the University specialized in the study of Mahāyāna Buddhism it did not exclude the study of the works belonging to the eighteen other sects of Buddhism, nor of such Brahminical sacred and secular subjects as the Vedas, the Atharva Veda, हेतुविद्या (Logic), शब्दविद्या (Grammar &Philology) चिकित्साविद्या (medicine), सांख्य, योग, न्याय and the like.

Comparable to Nalanda in the freedom of its academic life and the variety and catholicity of its studies as described by Yuan Chwang, there was another seat of learning, the hermitage of the sage fear दिवाकर मित्र, described by Bāṇa in the VIIIth chapter of *Harṣacaritam*. To that solitary and sylvan surroundings in the depths of the Vindhya forest was attracted all the varied culture of the age.

However, in these accounts of educational institutions we have an indication of the literature and circle of knowledge available in that age. Brahmanas learnt the Veda treatises including आयुर्वेद, यजुर्वेद, सामवेद and अथर्ववेद – as stated by Yuan Chwang.

According to I-Tsing who travelled in India a little later than Yuan Chwang, after the preliminary grounding in सिद्धवस्तु i.e. Sih-ti-chang Grammar and Composition with पाणिनि-सूत्रs, धातुs, काशिकावृत्ति, the students could proceed to a study of five subjects or Vidyas (both Yuan Chwang and I-Tsing are of same opinion) viz.

 i. शब्दविद्या – Sih-ti-chang i.e. Grammar and Lexicography.
 ii. शिल्पस्थानविद्या – Kiau-ming, the science of the Arts and Crafts.
 iii. चिकित्साविद्या – Medicine.
 iv. हेतुविद्या – Logic.
 v. अध्यात्मविद्या – Metaphysics.

So the third *vidyā* is called चिकित्साविद्या or the medical treatise which embraces formulae for protection, secret charms, the use of medicinal stones, acupuncture and mugwort or herbal medicine etc.

From '*Records of western countries*', we come to know,

«*Every one who falls sick fasts for seven days. During this interval many recover, but if the sickness lasts they take medicine. The character of these medicines is different and their names also. The doctors differ in their modes of examination and treatment*».

Before focussing out attention on the central theme of our paper, a few remarks concerning the history of medical science upto the age of Bana in particular would not be out of place here.

It goes without saying that the elements of medical science including surgery, were known even in the ṛgvedic times. This appears to be attested by some passages in RV praising Rudra and Surya as healers (RV II/334 and 1.55). The Aśvina brothers are said (1/116/10) to have rejuvenated Cyavana. Besides, they provided an iron thigh to Viśpalā who lost that limb (1/116.15).

सद्योजङ्घामायसीं विश्पलायै
धने हिते सर्तवे प्रत्यधत्तम् ॥

Viśpalā was, an amazon i.e. a female soldier who lost her limb in a war. Moreover these brothers are referred to have cured blindness and leprosy (RV I/112/8, X/39/3).

याभिः शचीभिः वृषणा परावृजं
प्रान्धं श्रोणं चक्षसः एतवे कृथः ॥

In the branch of medical science, Sanskrit has a very rich literature the fame of which spread beyond the boundaries of this peninsula specially in South and South East Asia in ancient times.

The main medical treatises in Sanskrit are the *Caraka – saṃhitā* (1st Cen. AD), *Suśruta-saṃhitā* (perhaps contemporaneous with Caraka). *Bhela saṃhitā, Aṣṭāṅgasamgraha, Rugviniścaya* or *Nidāna* of Madhava (who flourished probably in the 7th Cen. A.D). *Rasaratnākara, Rasaratnasamuccaya* etc. Of medical dictionaries, noteworthy are *Dhanvantari-nighaṇṭu, śabdapradīpa, Rājanighaṇṭu* etc.

Apart from some rare books on medical science the information about medical science contained in the *Purāṇas* is rather exhaustive. Agni-Purāṇa (hereafter AP). and Garuda – Purāṇa (hereafter GP). deserve special mention in this context.

It is believed that the Purāṇas are 36 in no; of these, 18 are Mahapurāṇas and 18 Upa – purāṇas. The Puranic literature appears to have originated before 5th or 4th century B.C. The extant Purāṇas appear to have come into being before 7th Century A.D.

Now the Purāṇas contain invaluable materials for reconstruction of the early political history, of geography, and many more aspects of ancient India. For history. of medical science in Ancient India, especially of 7th century the importance of Purāṇas can't be denied.

A.P. is encyclopaedic in character and deals with the following subjects.

1. Geography
2. Astronomy
3. Astrology
4. Marriage and death
5. Customs
6. Omens and portents
7. House building
8. Iconography
9. Usages of daily life

10. Politics
11. Art of war
12. **Medicine**
13. Metrics
14. Poetics
15. Grammar
16. Lexicography.

GP is also an encyclopaedic work dealing with

1. Rāmāyaṇa, Mahābhārata, Harivaṃśa,
2. Cosmography,
3. Astronomy,
4. Astrology,
5. Palmistry,
6. **Medicine**,
7. Metrics,
8. Grammar,
9. Precious stones

and many more subjects. A considerable portion of the याज्ञवल्क्य स्मृति is included in it.

Again we come back to the central theme of our paper. Ample references to Medical Science scattered all over Harṣacaritam are our present concern.

In Ch. I of HC, Bāṇa refers to

1. Opthalmic diseases:

त्रेताग्नि – धूमाश्रुपातजलक्षालितइवाक्षीयन्त कुदृष्टयः ॥

In Chapter IV while delineating the valour of a Bāṇa says

तेषु चैवमुत्पद्यामानेषु क्रमेणोदपादि हुण-हरिण-केसरी, सिन्धुराज-ज्वरो गुर्जर प्रजागरो, गान्धाराधिप-गन्धद्विप कूटपाकलः

कूटपाकलः is a dreaded disease common to elephants.

"कूटो नामाशुघातनमाशुघातनं द्विरदानाम्
तस्मात् कूटपाकलम् आचक्षस्महे इति"

प्रभाकरवर्द्धन was very much intimidating to his enemies just like a very lion to the deer in the form of Hunas; just like a कूटपाकलः disease to the elephants.

गन्धद्विप is an elephant of the best type; 'पाकलः' is a fever which attacks elephants; 'कूट' is one of the varieties and it is the deadliest of all.

Other references to the diseases of horses and elephants are found scattered in Harṣacaritam.

Bāṇa says प्रभाकरवर्द्धन was as dreadful as 'ज्वर' to 'सिन्धु' king. According to GP. the words रोग, पाम्मा, ज्वर, व्याधि, विकार, दुष्टम्, आमय, आतङ्क, गद, वाधा, यक्ष्मा are all synonyms of sickness.

In the Medical Science of Ancient India, 'ज्वर' or fever has been repeatedly mentioned with great importance. Since fever is the manifestation of many diseases, it should be considered very carefully, 'ज्वर' is occasionally identified with 'यक्ष्मा'. Caraka categorically says fever is curable if it is not very complicated and if it appears in persons having sufficient bodily strength to fight it out.

In certain cases the fever or 'ज्वर' may turn to be fatal.

"हेतुभिर्बहुभिर्जातो बलिभिर्बहुलक्षणः ।
ज्वरः प्राणान्तकृद् यश्च शीघ्रमिन्द्रियनाशनः ॥"

Caraka-saṃhitā /Cikitsāsthāna

Besides in 4th chapter, of HC यशोमती has beautifully been described with her pallor, with her slow and restricted movement, her hard breathing, slightly pallid body, dark nipples of her breasts due to pregnancy. Again Yaśomatī has been vividly shown as having a number of lady attendants.

i.   सख्युत्सङ्गमुक्तशरीरा च शरीरपरिचारिकाणामङ्केषु सपत्नीनां तु शिरःसु पादौ चकार ।
ii.   आत्मोचिततस्थाननिषण्णाश्च महान्तो विविधोषधिधरभिषजो भूधरा इव भूवो धृतिं चक्रुः ।

A group of veteran surgeons or doctors were keeping continuous vigilance and were ready with different kind of remedial medicines during the time of यशोमती's delivery.

In 4ᵗʰ ch. when प्रभाकरवर्द्धन was sounding cautions to his sons against swindlers, Bāṇa uses उन्मादरोग as उपमान

गीत-नृत्य-हसितैः उन्मत्तताम् आवहन्ति उपेक्षिता विकारा इव वातिका etc.

Just as वातिक or imbalance of वात, or wind leads to उन्माद रोग or insanity, so also धूर्त्त if they are ignored become much harmful to the kings.

It will not be irrelevant to mention here, that the 'pivot' round which the Indian medical science revolved is the conception that the body is preserved and guided by the three vital elements viz. wind (वात), bile (पित्त) and mucus (कफ). The body is fit when these are in a balanced condition. Due to the imbalance of these three humours, (त्रिदोष), the body becomes vulnerable to the attack of diseases. To these three i.e. वात, पित्त and कफ some added a fourth viz. blood.

When हर्षवर्द्धन was coming back to the capital he found some servants who were sitting outside धवलगृह and they were discussing the symptoms of the incurable disease. Someone, among the servants sitting outside, laid bare the errors on the part of the doctors.

केनचित्चिकित्सकदोषानुद्घावयता।
केनचित्साध्य-व्याधिलक्षणपदानि पठता॥

In Medical Science of ancient India, diseases are generally classified into three classes, साध्या, दुःसाध्य and असाध्य i.e.

1. curable
2. difficult to be cured/not easily curable
3. incurable,

Perhaps प्रभाकरवर्द्धन's disease was of third type and as such

The medical literature of ancient India was divided into eight principal branches –

1. शल्यतन्त्र – major surgery
2. शालाक्यतन्त्र – minor surgery (diseases of the eye, ear and other parts of the head)
3. कायचिकित्सा – therapeutics
4. भूतविद्या – demonology
5. कुमारविद्या – pediatrics
6. अगमतन्त्र or अगदतन्त्र – toxicology pertaining to poison
7. रसायन – elixir or cure-all remedy
8. वाजीकरणतन्त्र – aphrodisiac pertaining to sexual diseases.

In HC we find unlike other physicians रसायन who was the house-physician and who 'कुलक्रमागतो गतः पारम् अष्टाङ्गस्य आयुर्वेदस्य,' who was cherished by प्रभाकरवर्द्धन on the same footing as a son, the young man by his profound study of the science of medicine understood that the king would not live for more than a day. 'असोऽब्रवीत्-देव। श्वः प्रभाते यथावस्थितमावेदयितास्मि'।

Diseases were classified into four categories

i. Organic e.g. fever, (Tumor, Cancer may be included) leprosy (शारीरा)
ii. Mental e.g. anger, envy, Insanity (मानसा)
iii. Extraneous e.g. agantuka, Emergency wound (आगन्तुक)
iv. Functional e.g thirst, any kind of *inflammatory fever*, Diabetes (सहजा), malfunctioning of Thyroid etc. It has been stated in AP the diagnosis of diseases consist of five essential categories. शारीर-मानसा-गन्तु-सहजा व्याधयो मताः शारीरा ज्वरकुष्ठाद्याः सहजाः क्षुज्ज्वरादयः । A.P 280/1-2

The pathology of diseases falls into five categories, viz.

i. पूवरूपो – precursor or incurbatory stage
ii. रूप – symptoms
iii. उपशम – amelioration (improvement)
iv. शमप्राप्ति – location
v. विज्ञान – diagnosis (रोगनिर्णय)

Now this paper will show how Bāṇa quite conversant with both the theoretical and practical aspects of Indian Medical Science, gave a detailed and true account of the symptoms, remedial measures, amelioration, dietetics, diagnosis and many more aspects of Indian medical science while delineating king Prabhākaravardhana in his deathbed at Dhavalagrha and how the said factors are very much relevant in modern world also.

However, it has already been stated according to the medical science, diseases are originated through the imbalance of the bodily humours, which disturbs the state of their equillibrium.

The mdoe of this pathology differs with the differences of the prevailing season, number, nature, strength, predominance or neutrality of different morbific principles involved.

Śvāsa (Dyspnoea) is caused by chronic or aggravated cough or the morbific principles of the body. Exposure to dust, storm, smoke, cold wind blow on vulnerable points of nerves, arteries, vomitting, mucous dyscentry, fever, poisoning etc. are causes. (GP. 154, 1-8). Initial symptoms are acute pain about the heart and the sides, contrary direction of breathwind, long-drawn breath, pain at temporal bones and tympanites. (कर्णपटह). Five types of श्वास e.g. क्षुद्रक, तमक, छिन्न, महन्, ऊर्ध्वश्वास are enumerated in Indian medical science.

From the symptoms of the disease of Prabhākaravardhana it may clearly be interpreted that he had been suffering from महाश्वास combined with महाहिक्का as nomenclatured in Medical Science. Though these names were not found anywhere in ch. V. of HC but the symptoms of both the diseases were very much prominent in the description of the ailing king.

Symptoms of महाश्वास are – suppressed stool and urine, dry throat and mouth, hard and rapid respiration, drops of sweat on forehead, severe pain in head and temples, finally death.

There are five kinds of 'hiccough' enumerated as अन्नज, क्षुद्र, यमल, महाहिक्का and गम्भीर of which symptoms of महाहिक्का are Drooping eyebrows, unconsciousness, new pain in all sense organs, pain at heart, yawning and spasmodic jerks in limbs.

Almost all the symptoms are depicted for प्रभाकरवर्धन at his death-bed. The symptoms prescribed in the medical texts may not resemble exactly but we can find a remarkable similarity in the manifestation of the disease of प्रभाकरवर्द्धन. The symptoms identified in Harṣacarita are as follows –

1. Severe pain throughout the body including head and temples. As it is said by Bāṇa

    a. अनवरतपरिवर्तनै: H. C.-V, P-23
    b. अङ्ग-भङ्ग-वलनोत्क्षिप्तभुजयुगलम्: H. C.-V, P-23
    c. ग्रासीकृतमिव गात्रभङ्गेन: H. C.-V, P-23
    d. वट्यमानमिव वेदनाभि: H. C.-V, P-23

    प्रभाकरवर्द्धन was languishing in pain in all the organs; he had breaking of limbs. The stiffness of body has been repeatedly indicated.

2. The inflamation of the veins is indicated in the following statement: –

    a. दुर्धरवेदनो-न्नमन्-नीलशिराजालक-करालेन... H. C.-V, P-23

3. He heaved hot breaths; he had hard and rapid respiration as indicated by the following–

    a. मृगतृष्णिकामिव उष्णां निःश्वास-परम्परामुद्वहन्तम्: H. C.-V, P-23
    b. सततं श्वासिते... H. C.-V, P-23

4. He had a dark tongue, which indicated that he was in the stage of सन्निपात। सन्निपात is the combined derangement of the three humours of the body वात, पित, कफ causing fever which is of a dangerous kind and is fatal It is said.

    "श्यामायमानया रसनया निवेद्यमान – दारुण-सन्निपातारम्भम्)»

तन्द्रिक, one variety of सन्निपातज्वर is described as follows in योगरत्नाकर

«प्रभूता तन्द्रार्तिर्ज्वरकक्षपिपासाकुलतरो भवेच्छयामा जिह्वा पृथुलकठिना कन्टकवृता» etc.

5. High body-temperature of the King is described again and again

   a. ज्वरज्वलनेन,... H. C.-V, P-23

   b. अत्युष्ण-अवयव-स्वर्श-भस्मीभूत, H. C.-V, P-23

6. Dry throat and mouth as indicated by

   a. शुष्कास्यवाजि, etc. H. C.-V, P-23

7. Frequent yawning is indicated by जितं जृम्भिकाभिः..., H. C.-V, P-23

8. Occasional unconsciousness is indicated by स्पृशन्तीं प्रणयिनीमिव विश्वासभूमिं मूर्च्छामपि वहुमन्यमानम् meaning the king welcomed a swoon when it came over him, because it was a source of relief.

Now the remedial measures of the above-mentioned symptoms are described as follows:

Relief for the dry mouth & throat was made-

अनुजीवि-पाय्यमानोच्चषक-धारा वारिविनोद्यमाना-आस्यरुजि, H. C.-V, P-23

It is common experience that thirst is allayed much more quickly if one pours a stream of water into the mouth than if one holds the cup to the lips. According to the translation of prof Cowell and Mr. Thomas *"attendants were drinking streams of water from uplifted cups in order to distract the pain of the king's dry mouth."* But following Paṇḍit P. V. Kane we would like the reading पाय्यमान for पीयमान 'would be' where the pain of the dry mouth (of the king) was removed by streams of water (without cups) which he was made to drink by the attendants. पाय्यमान reading is more comfortable since it is not practical that how the king's dry mouth would have been relieved if the servants drank water! Moreover, उच्चषकम् अपगतपानभाजनम् don't mean 'empty cups' but rather without a cup. However, the reading उच्चषकम् is better.

Thus the full sentence should stand as follows

अनुजीवि-पाय्यमान-उच्च-चषक-धारा-वारि विनोद्यमाना-आस्यरुजि-

which means that the water was poured from a cup held high up and not from a cup applied to the lips. This can easily remind one of 'Feeding cup' used for the patients in the Hospitals etc.

मस्तु i.c. whey in Bengali माटा तोला घोल, वा छानार जल

नाश्यान-पङ्क-लिप्यमान-नव-भाण्डगत-गण्डूप-ग्रहण-मस्तुनि H. C.-V, P-23

The cool whey was probably required for relieving the dryness of mouth of the patient who used it as a gargle from time to time.

मुहुर्मुहु-राहूयमान-तोय-कर्मान्तिक-अनुमित-घोरातुरतृषि H. C.-V, P-22, meaning a servant was being called upon frequently to supply water to give some relief to the dry throat and the mouth of the king.

तुषार परिकरित-करक-शिशिरीक्रियमाण उदश्विति – where buttermilk (घोल in Bengali) was being cooled (frozen) in jars (करक कमण्डलु) that were covered in ice. उदश्वित् is buttermilk that contains 50 percent water (तक्रं हृदश्विन्मथितं) which reminds one of application of icebag whatsoever. The frozen buttermilk was probably applied to the burning feet and head of feverish king which can easily remind one of the application of ice-bag or pouring of water on the head of the patient in the medical treatment of modern age also.

The lotus leaves, fibres and flowers were all used to produce a cooling effect. It is said सनाल-नीलोत्पल-पूली-सनाथ सलिलपान-भाजनभुवि... H. C.-V, P-22 श्वेतार्द्र-कर्पटार्पित-कर्पूर-पराग-शीतलीकृत-शलाके (श्वेतार्द्रे कर्पटे (piece of cloth) अर्पिताः कर्पूरस्य परागाः तेन शीतलीकृता शलाका यस्मिन्) The stick treated with camphor powder was to be applied to the eye to produce a cooling effect.

The importance of taking water is always stressed in Indian medical Science. It is said –

कुक्षे भर्गिद्वयं भोज्यैस्तृतीये वारि पुरयेत् ।
वायोः सञ्चरणार्थाय चतुर्थमवशेषयेत् ॥

It will not be out of place to mention that sealed drinking water was brought for emperors.

In order to reduce body temperature lotus-petals, sandalwood-paste were being applied very requently.

In order to quench the thirst, water was being supplied regularly and in order to make it free from the germs water was first boiled and then cooled and thus the germfree water, first boiled and then cooled was provided for a patient for drinking even in those days also. Bāṇa says

धारा निपात-निर्बाप्यमान-क्वथिताम्भसि H. C. V. P.22.

निबिड़-दुकूल-पट्ट-निपीड़ित — केशान्त-कथ्यमान-कष्टवेदनानुबन्धं मूधींनं धारयन्तम् Pravhākara-vardhana's. head was bound tight with silk cloth around the skull because he was suffering from ceaseless headache and balm was being applied on his forehead. प्रेष्या-पेष्यमाण-ललाट केपो-उपदग्ध-हृषदि etc. H. C. V. P.-22.

Now, there is remarkable similarity between the diet and medicine prescribed by the medical texts and the same provided for the king.

It is said in the Agnipurāṇa –

कैलत्थ-मौद्रको-रास्ना – शुष्कमूलक-जाङ्गलै:
पूपैर्वा विष्किरै: सिद्धै – दंधिदाड़िम-साधितै:
मातुलुङ्गरस-क्षौद्र-द्राक्षाव्योषादि-संस्कृतै:
यव-गोधूम-शाल्यन्नै-भोजयेत्-श्वास-कासिनम् AP. 279/20,21.

However, 'Dietetics' was a very deveoped branch of study in Indian medical Science. It is sad in पथ्यापथ्यम् ।

"विनापि भेषजैव्याधि पथ्यादेव निवर्त्तते
न तु पथ्यविहीनानां भेषजानां शतैरपि "

A disease can be cured fully by proper diet and on the other hand, the application of hundreds of medicines are useless without proper diet.

However, in H. C we find Harṣa entered the inner court smelling the odour of boiling decoctions of butter and oils that were being heated.

विविधौ-षधि-द्रव-गन्ध-गर्भम् उत्क्वथतां क्वाथानां सर्पिषां तैलानां च प्रपच्यमानानां गन्धमजिघ्रन्नवाप तृतीयं कक्ष्यान्तरम्। H. CV, P-22

In medical text, Diet for treatment of Śvāsa is prescribed as कुलत्थ and मुद्र pulses prepared with rāsnā, curd, honey, juice of मातुलुङ्ग, grapes, wheat, barley or boiled शालि rice and Decoction of ginger and शर्करा or sugar etc. Besides, long pepper, sugar, ginger with honey are prescribed for treatment of 'hiccough' too.

शर्करा both white and red are mentioned in H. C too while describing धवलगृह

    a.   पटुपाटलशर्करा आमोदमुचि H. C.-VP-22
    b.   मसार-पारी-परिगृहीत-कक4-शकरे H. C.-V, P-22

A paste of flour and curds was held in a yellow emerald cup.

शिशिरोषध-रस-चूर्णावकीर्ण-स्फटिक-शक्ति-शङ्ख-सञ्चये H. C.-V, P-22

Moreover, myrobalans (आमलकि), grapes were stored. The myrobalans are said to be very much effective for removing the three 'doṣas' (त्रिदोष) i.e वात, पित्त, कफ। 'मातुलुङ्ग' citron according to P. V. Kane, it resembles Marathi महालुंग. However, मातुलुङ्ग may be identified with मौसाम्वी as we call it in Bengali.

महाश्वास and महाहिक्का both are said to be incurable diseases finally leading only to the death and that is why Rasāyaṇa, the then renowned medical practitioner never gave any hope for survival of प्रभाकरबर्द्धन। When asked by Harsa –

"रसायन कथय तथ्यं यदि असाधु इव पश्यसि" (H. C. VP-25) Rasāyaṇa avoided the direct reply and answered "देव, श्व:, प्रभाते यथावस्थितम् आवेदयितास्मि (H. C. V P-25). On the next day Rasāyaṇa, of noble birth preferred entering fire than conveying unwelcome and distressing words of king's impending death.

Bāṇa repeatedly hinted at the last journey of प्रभाकरबर्द्धन using a number of beautiful but poignant expressions.

i.   परलोकविजयाय नीराज्यमानमिव a i.e Fever was the fire and the king was about to proceed as it were to the next world and was performing religious ceremony or नीराजना. Other similar expressions are as follows: –

ii.   क्षयकाले शुष्यन्तम् H. C.-V, P-23

iii.   लोकान्तरप्रस्थितम् H. C.-V, P-23

iv.   कालकटाक्षपतनशबलमिव शरीरमुद्वहन्तम् H. C.-V, P-23

v.   महाप्रस्थानकाले... सञ्चारयन्तम् H. C.-V, P-23

vi.   कालेन क्रोड़ाकृतम् H. C.-V, P-23

vii.   दैवेन आदित्सितम् H. C.-V, P-23

viii.   निरूपितं नियत्या H. C.-V, P-23

ix.   परिकलितं परासुतया H. C.-V, P-22

x.   मुखे महाप्रवासस्य H. C.-V, P-22

अन्तिकेऽन्त्य उच्छ्वासस्य who was near the last breath, who was broken in words – विरलं वाचि प्रचुरप्रलापे profuse in incoherent speech, was waiting his last breath.

Thus from the above deliberation it can fairly be concluded that during 7th century A. D. Indian medical science was in a appreciably developed stage which was evident from the classification of diseases, symptoms, dietitics, application of medicines diagnosis etc. as reflected in Bāṇabhaṭṭa's Harṣacaritam, an outstanding work of highest literary value, in the portrayal of प्रभाकरवर्द्धन at his deathbed.

पश्यत्वार्थः क्व परमाणुपरिमाणं वटुहृदयम्
क्व समस्तब्रह्मस्तम्भव्यापि देवस्य चरितम्
क्व परिमित-वर्णवृत्तयः कतिपये शब्दाः
क्व संख्यातिगास्तद्गुणाः,

Bāṇa himself said, "it is daring to attempt delineation of Harsha's character with such a limited capability, so as to describe his all-pervading actions with a few sentences or words."

I would like to conclude with the same spirit, "*every details relating to only one aspect of Bāṇa's work with my limited capability as well as within this short span of time, the capability is as small as that of an atom, is quite impossible.* In spite of that

तथापि नृपतेर्भक्त्या भीतो निर्वहणाकुलः ।
करोम्याख्यायिकाम्भोधो जिह्वाप्लवनचापलम् ॥

«*Through my devotion to my king (Harṣa), being undismayed and eager to carry out (my undertaking) make bold to plunge with my tongue in the ocean of* आख्यायिका।»

In the same spirit, I would like to say through my strong devotion to Bāṇabhaṭṭa and eagerness to refresh myself and to refresh you i.e all the participants too I have made a humble attempt to plunge with my 'pen' in the ocean of 'हर्षचरितम्' ।

Abbreviations Used:

AP – Agnipurāṇam, edt. By Tarkaranath, Calcutta, 1389 BS 1ˢᵗ ed.

GP – Garuḍapurāṇa, edt. By Tarkaranath, Calcutta, 1392 BS 1ˢᵗ ed.

HC – The Harṣacharita of Bāṇabhaṭṭa, edt. By P.V. Kane, 1917, Bombay

Bibliography:

Agnipurāṇam	- edt. By Tarkaratna, Calcutta, 1389 BS
Āyurveda in Classical Sanskrit Literature	- A. Mukhopadhyay, Kolkata, 2004
Bengal's contribution to Sanskrit Literature	- K. K. Dutta, Calcutta, 1974
Companion to Sanskrit Literature	- Banerjee 2ⁿᵈ ed. 1989, Delhi 1ˢᵗ ed. 1971
Gangadhara Kaviraja	- Rita Chattopadhyay, Calcutta, 1995
Garuḍapurāṇa	- edt. By Tarkaratna, Calcutta, 1406 (Reprint), 1392 (1ˢᵗ. ed)

Harṣa – (Ancient Indian
Tradition and Mythology series) - Radhakumud Mukherjee
Harṣacarita   - ed. Thakur, 1986
Harṣacarita   - Cowell, 2nd ed., 1st ed. 1978
(The) Harṣacarita of
Bāṇabhaṭṭa   - ed. P.V. Kane, Bombay, 1917
Harṣacarita (v)   - ed. Pandeya, Chowkhamba
                                    Vidhyabhavan, 1984

Khādyatattva o
Pathyavicār   - (W.B.) Majumdar, Calcutta, 1348
                                    BS

Prācin Bhārate
Cikitsāvijñān (in Bengali)   - Debi Prasad Chattopadhyay. Cal.
                                    1996, (reprint), 1st ed. 1992.

Journals :
Anvīkṣā   - Vol. XXIII, 2001
Jāhnavī   - Rajat Jayanti Samkhyā, 1404 BS.

[*Note* – This paper was published in *Anvīkṣā Journal* Vol – XXVI, March 2005, Page – 13]

False Yogi (Translation)

Bengali Drama – Kapat Sadhu – by Sri Archana Puri
(Translated by – *Prof. Rita Chattopadhyay)*

(This playlet is based on the popular and interesting story, repeatedly and inspiringly narrated by Sree Ramakrishna Paramahamsadeva, bearing some deep philosophical truth. It projects the Truth that samsara, i.e., the bondage of wordly life and Mukti, freedom from that bondage – both depend on 'His' will only. The present drama shows how even a pretended piety can transform a sinner to a saint and make his life blessed by causing his spiritual upliftment.)

Scene I

(The orchard of wealthy Amarnath. Amarnath is sitting alongwith his friends.)

First friend – Amarnath, how beautiful your orchard is! Last year we were lucky enough to get the fruits of your garden. But what's wrong? This year we are deprived of the same?

Amar – Brothers! What can I say? I am very much worried. The fruits are stolen from my orchard. Not just that, but also the fishes from the pond.

Second friend – Really! Then truly it's a matter of great concern. Dear Amar! You have to strengthen the security. Otherwise, who will prevent the theft of goods inside the house alongwith the fruit and the fish?

Amar – Brother! One guard and one gardener are already there.

First friend – Oho! The guard and the gardener! Now the whole matter is clear as crystal. You are bringing up thieves inside your very house. As such thieving can never be checked here.

Amar – But, you know, they are working from the days of my father. They are exceedingly loyal.

First friend – Brother! Who can guarantee that a saint in your father's time will not turn into a thief during his son's days.

Amar – Please, suggest me Brothers. What should I do now?

Second friend – Don't worry; we will do the needful. Let us engage some village-boys to guard your orchard and let us now see whether the thief is apprehended or not.

Amar – Thank you Brothers! Please do the same. There is no other alternative.

Scene II

(Dark night. A corner of the garden. A thief enters surreptitiously with a fishing net in his hand. He looks around.......)

Thief – I can neither see the watchman nor the gardener anywhere. This place seems to be absolutely deserted. Yet sounds can be heard from that side. Any way there is no need to go there, I shall return with a few catches in the pond. I should be satisfied with whatever little 'He' bestows on me.

(Now the thief tosses the net and begins fishing)

(Other corner of the orchard. The boys are conversing with one another)

First – Brother! Do you hear? Some sound can be heard from that side – is not it?

Boys (altogether) – Who's there? Who's there?

Second boy – Oh No! Not that side. The sound is heard in this side only.

Other boy – No, No! Not that side brother! It can be heard from the other side. Let us go through the winding path below the mango tree. I am quite sure that someone is there.

(The boys begin to search everywhere)

Thief – Goddam, I hear many voices. What shall I do now?

(Other corner of the Orchard)

Boys – Let some of us surround the orchard lest the thief should escape. We will keep a watch on this side.

Thief – What luck! There is no escaping now. I will surely be caught now. Oh God! deliver me.

(The thief looks around, while trying to escape suddenly falls in a heap of ashes.)

Thief – Ah! Here is a heap of ashes. This is fine. Let me smear my body and face completely with the ashes. Now I shall sit here under the tree in a saint's guise.

(The thief feigns meditation in Yogi's guise. The boys who were in search of the thief observe him from a distance).

First friend – Oho! I see a shadowy figure near the pond. But the place is very dark. Let us go with a torch.

Second friend – Be careful. Take the rod along with you. Otherwise, if the thief has any sort of weapon there will be danger.

(The boys come in front of the thief in disguise of a saint.)

First boy – Oh look! He is not a thief. A great Yogi is meditating here. What an accident it would have been! If we had struck him how tragic it would be. Thank God, we've brought the torch.

Second boy – Anyway, God has saved us. Thank God, we are not instrumental in murdering a holy man. Come along, let us beg for his mercy.

(All bow down before the Yogi.)

Second boy – Oh Maharaj (Baba)! Unknowingly we were about to hit you. Prabhu! Forgive us all.

(Yogi pretended meditation and remained standstill.)

First boy – Look! He is static like a piece of wood. Come along, we should not disturb his meditation. (Exit)

Scene III

(Next morning. The news spread that a great Yogi has arrived in the village. The villagers pour into the garden with fruit and flowers to have Darshan of the Yogi.)

First villager – Oh Maharaj! My only daughter is seriously ill. Kindly do something for her recovery.

(Yogi reassures him with the well-known gesture of blessing and give him a pinch of ashes.)

First – All Hail to Baba! All Hail to Maharaj!

Second – Baba, let me have better days. I barely live from hand to mouth. I can't bear it any more. Please bless me to have enough wealth to eat rice in the gold-vessel along with my grandson.

(Yogi raised his hand and blessed him and gave a pinch of ashes.)

Second – I am now sure to have better days. Who else is more lucky than myself?

Lady – Baba! I wish my daughter-in-law begets a bonny male child, who will carry on my succession. My husband passed away and didn't see his grandson. Would I have the same fate? Have pity on me. So that my daughter-in-law begets a male child.

(Yogi raised his hand in blessing and gave her a pinch of ashes.)

Lady – I will make an amulet out of this ashes and make my daughter-in-law wear it. Oh how kind my Master is! When my successor will come, I will request Yogi Maharaj for a holy visit to my hut.

Fourth man – Baba, a lawsuit has been filed in the court. Kindly bless me so that I can win. My brother is trying to grab my entire possession in illegal way. Let my brother turn into a pauper.

(Yogi raised his hand and blessed, gave a pinch of ashes.)

Fourth man – I will make an amulet out of this ashes and while going to the court I will put the amulet on my arm. Let me see how the enemy can defeat me. All Hail to Baba! All Hail to Baba!

Another devotee – Baba, everybody comes to you with some material desire. You assure them and bless them silently. But I have come to you with some other purpose. For 'whom' you have renunciated this worldly life, I want to renuntiate everything for 'Him'. I shall be a Yogi like you, a Yogi only, Baba, I am at your feet. Make me a Yogi.

Thief (Monologue) – What a miracle! I am not at all a holy man! On the contrary, I am an unholy thief. Last night I came here only with the purpose of thieving. I smeared myself completely with the ashes just to save my life and with closed eyes pretended to be a holy man, a Yogi. But in the light of the dawn all my sins have been washed away as it were. Everybody now comes to me for Darshan, they earnestly ask for my blessings and bring me fruits and flowers. None of them suspects my identity. I have only been pretending to be a holy man, and for that I am being honoured so much! If I turn into a saint, a holy man in reality, then certainly I shall attain 'His Love'. Then I shall have nothing of one's life. Oh God! You haven't punished me. The ardent devotion of these innocent people has turned my soiled soul into Gold.

Devotee – Prabhu! My Lord! Are you leaving now?

Thief – Yes my child, from now both of us will live in search of that 'Highest Treasure'.

Devotee – What is that 'Highest Treasure'?

Thief – God, that Almighty, who has opened my eyes, who has breathed into you the glow of renunciation. Let us, for 'Him', give up our worldly desires. We will be 'Yogi in reality'.

Devotee – Prabhu, why do you say so? What do you mean by 'Yogi in reality'?

Thief – I mean – Last night I was a 'False Yogi'. Now I am a 'True Yogi' in the real sense. A true Yogi, a real Yogi, a genuine Yogi.

(Ramakrishna Paramahansadeva is seen in the background.)

Ramakrishna – Now you see, this much consciousness has been awakened only with this fraudulent sadhana. Then what more to say if the sadhana is real?

(Curtain)

[*Note* – This Drama was published in *The Golden Horizon*, First year, First Issue, Monthly Bulletin of Sree Satyananda Devayatan, January 1994, Page – 7]

5

Modern Sanskrit Plays

A Glimpse into Tradition and Innovation

"काव्येषु नाटकं रम्यम्"
Drama[1] (Rūpaka/Nāṭaka) is the finest form of literary creation.

The terms 'modern' and 'Sanskrit might sound anachronistic to any casual reader so that even thinking of innovation in Sanskrit might seem inconsistent. Fortunately however, if there is one task that this paper wishes to accomplish, it is to resolve the apparent incompatibility between Sanskrit and a largely under-emphasized aspect of modernity in it. And the means to achieving that end is to journey through the vast realm of Sanskrit literature that are being composed now, getting glimpses of modern techniques and themes and witnessing the influences of current affairs on all genres. In this paper we begin our journey by taking the path through 'drama'.

'Drama' or 'Nāṭya[2]' is the finest form of literary creation. Drama is neither a static form of art, nor a motionless picture of the universe; but it reflects the dynamic nature of the world characterized by incessant flow of happiness and despair[3]. It is an active portrayal of the sentiments that revolve around us.

It goes without saying that every piece of art is necessarily a form of social consciousness. An artist is but a social being and a product of his or her social environment, which speaks through his/her creation. Be it the case of carvings of the caves or the more advanced form of artistic expression viz. poetry, drama, dance or so; each component and motive thereof come out of social urge. Portrait of Draupadi in the Mahābhārata, for instance, reflects a society where the woman-folk could hardly resist onslaughts of male chauvinism. Likewise, The Merchant of Venice by Shakespeare reveals an atmosphere of social hatred and animosity where the Jews were in no way on the same footing as the Christians. And in portraits of individual characters in social environment in novels by Bankim Chandra Chattopadhyay, Rabindra Nath Tagore, Sarat Chandra Chattopadhyay, Tarashankar Bandyopadhyay, Manik Bandyopadhyay, Narayan Gangopadhyay, Prem Chand, Mulkraj Anand and other Indian litterateurs too, we come to realize the inner truths of human existence in 19th / 20th century Indian context. It is not without reason that V.I. Lenin characterized Leo Tolstoy's Literature as the mirror of Russian revolution.

Verily, changes in social conditions usually lead to changes in art in respect of both content and form. The world scenario of Art of 20th century as it reflects the socio-economic tensions resulting in two devastating world wars and rise of new independent nations over the ashes of colonial powers is a case in point.

The Waste Land by T.S. Eliot at the backdrop of erosion of values in the great war, *Gītāñjali* (Songs of Offerings) by Tagore as a solace to the then-ailing humanity or for that matter *Sabhyatār Saṅkaṭ* (*Crisis in Civilization*) by him as a prophetic call to resurrection of soaring dignity of the human civilization amply testify to the complex network of relationship between society and art.

Recent developments in technocrafts have brought about a revolution in all art forms including literature. Literary pursuits have undergone a sea change to the tune of technological advancements so much so that even literary idioms including metaphor have adapted to computational devices in terms of precision and exactitude. Literary pursuits in any corner of the world now, in fact, are bound to react to global issues and phenomena.

Every language in a sense is a confluence. It enriches itself with whatever it comes across in course of its development and pays back in turn by contributing to their progress. And Sanskrit language is no exception here. For centuries together, Sanskrit has been enjoying the privilege of accommodating the vast pool of linguistic properties all over India to its fold and has been able to attain a really composite character.

It should be admitted on all hands that Sanskrit in generally recognized as the language of the Vedas. Purāṇas and the great classics of yore. Consequently contemporary Sanskrit writings suffer from a prevailing negligence. Still during 20th and 21st century A.D a large number of epics, short poems, dramas, sonnets, versical renderings in Sanskrit from other languages; prose-works e.g., essays, novels, short stories, etc. anthological works, works on poetics; works on grammar, works on different streams of sciences and hundred valuable commentaries have been produced in India.

In this background the present author through her present paper endeavoursto evince the fact how Sanskrit playwrights in the 20th Century, especially in the post-Independence period, through their literary works have made a thorough study of human society and of social relations and social changes, how they have used the literary idioms befitting the present time and modern taste, how they have handled themes thereof more down to earth than ethereal; how in the said works the innovations have prevailed upon traditionalism and conventionalism not only in respect of theme and technique but in respect of language too. Needless to say the above stated trends are traceable in other genres (e.g. short story, novel, poem etc.) also; but the plays only are our concern here.

It is to be mentioned here that in the present work 'Drama' or 'Play' is synonymous with Sanskrit '*Dṛśyakāvya*' or '*Nāṭya*' or with Bengali and Hindi *Nāṭaka*.

The statement made by Bharata regarding ' *Nāṭaka* ' – a special type of 'play', may safely be applied for *Nāṭya* or 'Play' in general.

Traditionally Sanskrit poetry (Kavya) has been classified broadly under two categoires[4] – *Dṛśyakāvya* and *Śravyakāvya*. Literally,

"दृश्यश्रव्यत्वभेदेन पुनःकाव्यं द्विधा मतम्"

"Kavyas are of two varieties – *Dṛśyakāvya* and *Śravyakāvya* «

Literarlly *Dṛśyakāvya* stands for a poetic composition where the aesthetic feeling and its taste (asvadana) arise through the act of witnessing[5] a drama.

The appeal to heart is communicated here through the visual sense-organ (darsanendriya).

Hence, in spirit, such compositions (*Dṛśyakāvya*) are different from the other variety i.e., *Śravyakāvya*, which appeals to the 'ear' i.e., sense-organ of hearing (*Śravyakāvya*). Thus *Śravyakāvya* [6] is a metrical composition or the like that can be heard only.

Whatever the position may be, for being considered as a *kāvya* both of these varieties of compositions (*Dṛśya* and *Śravya*) must have the singular characteristic of the creation of 'Rasa' in the absence of which both these varieties are liable to be eliminated from being enlisted in the category of *kāvya* [7a, 7b]. Thus the primary success of both of them lies in creating Rasa by rousing dormant passions (*sthāyibhāvas*) through the aesthetic representation or the art-communication.

Keeping 'all these aspects' in view the present author would like to evaluate the 20th and 21st Century Sanskrit plays with a focus on Bengal scenario.

But though in these modern centuries our Bengal's rather India's society has been subjected to a drastic change in almost all spheres of existence, though the old-world concepts of values are no longer valid; though the modern intellectuals find no utility of Sanskrit; yet, we have a considerable number of Paṇḍits – the real devoted and dedicated lovers of Sanskrit – who by their unrelenting effort kept the stream of Sanskrit still flowing and consequently a literature of high merit both qualitatively and quantitatively has been handed down to us.

During the period mentioned above a number of *Mahākāvyas, Khṇḍdakāvyas, Dūtakāvyas, Dṛśyakāvyas*[8], Sanskrit sonnets, versical renderings in Sanskrit from other languages have been produced in Bengal. Besides during this period, Sanskrit prose has achieved tremendous progress through essays, fictions e.g., novels, short stories etc. The stories especially translations from renowned Bengali works; anthological works, works on poetics, works on metrics; works on grammar, works on medical science and other streams of science too and hundreds of valuable commentaries on different branches of Sanskrit literature have been produced in Bengal. Some Sanskrit periodicals also have been published through the efforts of the Sanskritists of this region.

In the short span of this paper it has not been possible to give an analytical picture of the dramas, but an earnest attempt has been made to furnish at least some introductory notes, some special features thereon.

Since the number of Sanskrit Dramas produced under the said period is appreciably large i.e., more than 500 we are compelled to keep aside a good number of outstanding works outside the purview of our discussion for which we beg to be apologized by the learned scholars. The main intension here is to focus the perfect juxtaposition of tradition and innovation in the works concerned and to bring the so-long hidden talents into limelight.

Theme

Herein Sanskrit plays have been classified into seven categories. In each category some dramas have been introduced and at least one drama, by way of specimen, has been chosen to justify the theme of the paper i.e., perfect juxtaposition of tradition of innovation. In the process an attempt is made to touch upon some provinces of this vast peninsula, India, of course with a focus on Bengal.

Historical Plays

"नाटकं ख्यातवृत्तं स्यात"

"A *nāṭaka* (a drama) is a variety of *Rūpaka*,

wherein the subject-matter should be well-known."

In this category, more than sixty historical plays produced in this century have been traced of which some are based on the ancient period of Indian history e.g., on Candragupta Maurya, Asoka and so on; some historical dramas are based on medieval Indian history; some on the history of modern period e.g., on freedom movement of India, on Kashmir problem under the administration of Nehru and some on some important event of world history e.g., on the birth of a new nation – Bangladesh, Some of the historical plays are enumerated below.

धर्माशोकम् by Shanti Nath Ghosh ((Bengal) on the anecdote depicting how *Caṇḍāśoka* was transformed to *Dharmauoka*. It was staged on 1964, 2006, and 2007 and is scheduled to be performed at Kolkata on 3rd September, 2009.

सुभाषविजयम् *Subhāṣvijayam* by Nityananda of Bengal deals with the political career and stormy life of Netaji Subhas Chandra Bose popularly and widely known as Netaji and deals mainly with his prolonged fight with the British for the freedom of India. His supreme command over Indian National Army better known as Azad Hind Fauz, the march of INA through Burma, the series of brilliant rear-guard actions of INA in the jungles of Manipur and Burma with gallantry and skill are delineated in this play. But the late defeat of INA led by Netaji and surrender etc. have been avoided by the author.

अमरवीरवृत्तान्तम् by Nityananda of Bengal, deals primarily with the execution of Khudiram Bose, a patriot of 18 years only. All of us know that Khudiram along with Prafulla Chaki attempted to murder Mr. Kingsford, Chief Presidency Magistrate, Muzaffarpur (Bihar); they threw a bomb at a carriage which resembled that of Kingsford but really belonged to one Mr. Kennedy with the result that the wife and the daughter of the latter were killed. Khudiram was tried and hanged. He mounted the scaffold with his body erect and with a cheerful and smiling face and cried वन्दे मातरम्. Khudiram became heroes of folk songs sung all over the country. The last scene reminds us the famous song in Bengali.

एकवार विदाय दे मा घरे आसि /
आमि हासि हासि परव फांसि देखवे जगतवासी //

कटुविपाकः by Lila Rao Dayalu shows how the villagers of Gujrat were inspired by *Dāṇḍiyātra* and Civil Disobedience novement initiated by Gandhiji.

वीरभा by the same author shows how the women of the peasant class in Gujrat put forth their protest against "Land Settlement System" under the leadership of वीरभा, a staunch supporter of Mahatma Gandhi.

राष्ट्रबन्धु नाम by Matinath Mishra deals with the Freedom Movement with a focus on Gujrat chapter.

जयन्ती कुमायुनीयाः by Lila Rao Dyalu, portrays the skill in warfare and patriotism and valour of the soldiers from Kumaon during Indo-China war.

धन्योऽहं धन्योऽहं by G B Palsule on the patriotic activities of veer (Valiant) Savarkar.

देशबन्धु-देशप्रियम् by J.B. Chaudhuri, on the life of C.R. Das and Jatindra Mohan Sengupta, two great nationalists of Bengal.

Now some works on political issues either in international background or in national level;

some works on socio-political, socio-economic issues either in serious vein or with sarcasm will be mentioned.

ड्वातन्त्र्य-यज्ञाहुति (Sanskrit Ratnakara, 1956) a drama by Dr. Narayan Shastri Kankar of Jaipur, Rajasthan deals with 1942 movement.

अपूर्व-शान्ति-संग्राम and सत्याग्रहोदय by V. K. Chatre and Ramaliiga Shastri — both are on Satyagraha movement initiated by Mahatma Gandhi.

रक्ताभिषेकम् one act play by Abhiraja Rajendra Mishra is based on the problem of Khalistan.

सिन्धु-सौवीर-संग्रामम् this is a play by Srijiva Nyayatirtha of Bengal based on the Kashmir problem.

बांलादेशोदयम् (Delhi, 1972, 1st ed. 1988, 2nd ed.) by Ram Krishna Sharma is a 10 – act play

dealing with one of the most important events of recent history, the birth of a new nation i.e., Bangladesh out of what was, East Pakistan. The play with 10-acts is a faithful portrayal of historical events and historical characters e.g. Yahya Khan, the Pakistani General; of Zulfikar Ali Bhutto, the Pakistani political leader, of Sheikh Mujibur Rahaman, the Bangladeshi political leader and the leader of Awami league.

The playwright seems to be in his best in the last *śloka*, which is a *Bharatavākya* where Mujib wishes deep friendship between India and Bangladesh and expresses hope for communal harmony between the Hindu and the Muslim.

गङ्गा-यमुना यावद् बङ्ग-सिन्धु-हिमालयौ
बङ्ग-भारतयोः मैत्री तावत् स्थास्यति भूतले ।
स्वाधीना स्मो वयंत्वद्य स्वश्रमफलभोगिनः
गीता-कुराणयोः पाठम् कुर्यास्मः सहिता सदा ॥

बांलादेशविजयम् – (*Saṃskṛta-Pratibhā*) by Padma Shstri of Uttarpradesh is almost on the same theme. It deals primarily with the struggle of *Mukti-vāhini* under the guidance of Mujib. The gods like Narada, Indra and so on are introduced as visualizing the Bangladesh War from upper atmospheric region and ultimately the drama ends with the blessings of Narada, "Bangladesh will be a free country".

कांग्रेसपराभवम् (Pubd. 1977), (The defeat of the Congress), is a 10 – act play by Reba Prasad Dwivedi of Madhya pradesh. Indira Gandhi's appeal to the Supreme Court against the verdict of Allahabad High Court, the defeat of Congress party led by Mrs. Gandh, the victory of Janata

Dal under the leadership of Morarji Desai in 1977 election have been wonderfully tackled as theme.

वालेश्वरमहायुद्धम् (Mans). – (V.M.) is a drama in five acts written by pt. Nityananda Smrtitirtha of Bengal (1987/1988 A. D.). This drama deals with the patriotic activities of Jatindranath Mukherjee (8.12.1879-10.9.1915) widely known as *"Baghajatin"* of Bengal and specially with the *Baleswar* fight where sacred martyrdom of Bagha Jatin was gloriously held. V.M. a fine book, which with simple style and diction not only testifies to the author's deep grounding in Sanskrit language but also his fine literary talent.

The death of hero, though a notable and remarkable departure from convention, yet the success of the play lies in the message of the primary import of lying down Yatindra's life unhesitatingly to free his motherland from the shackle of imperialism. Though it is mentioned in the dramaturgical text *vadho yuddham…caibhir varjitah* etc., "वधो युद्धं … चैभिर्वर्जितः" SD/VI still innovation is found in representation of the hero's death – of course a new dimension has been given; a novel perspective can easily be traced.

Biographical plays

"इतरद्वा सदाश्रयम्"

"Biographical literature[9] is an important and significant sector of Modern Sanskrit Literature."

Internationally significant religious and spiritual figures like Śankaracharya, Ramakrishna, Vivekananda: political personalities like Mahatma Gandhi, Paṇḍit Nehru, Lokamanya Tilak, Rajendra Prasad, Churchill, Dr. Bidhan Ch. Roy, Indira Gandhi; popular saints and mystics e.g. Jñāneśvara, Ramdasa, Tukaram and well known scholars like Max Muller; Rabindranath Tagore have become the subject of biographical dramas.

Actually, writing Biographical dramas on historical personalities, is undoubtedly a very difficult task. Biographical work should neither be a mere history or biography i.e. an insipid statement of dates and facts nor can it be a mere 'fiction' or 'fantasy' soaring only on the wings of imagination however, sweet or charming. Thus an author of biographical literature – be it either in poetic or in dramatic form – has to steer between two extremes; history and imagination, cautiously but artistically. Thus the proper and perfect synthesis of history and literary art; truth and fiction lies at the root of the success of a Biographical play. In this category also we have come across more than sixty (60) dramas. To name a few: –

भास्करोदयम् This is a novel biographical drama of mahanataka type, in 15 acts, based on the early life (up to 25th year) of Poet Rabindranath Tagore, written by Dr. Jatindra Bimal Chaudhuri of Bengal published by 'Pracyavani', Calcutta in 1961.

The language of this drama is a unique one and captures the hearts of the connoisseurs. The language is simple yet dignified; true to the point yet sweet; modern, yet following the traditional rules. Some portions of speeches, poems and songs of Rabindranath, have been wonderfully and successfully rendered into Sanskrit, retaining to a large extent, the cadence, spirit and sublimity of the original.

तुकारामचरितम् Originally written in form of poetry by Kshama Rao in 1950: later on dramatized by Lila Rao. Act play dealing with the life and spiritual activities of the great poet, saint and devotee, 'Tukarama', (C. 1608-49 A.D.) of Maharashtra.

लोकमान्यस्मृतिः by S.B. Velankar, Maharashtra. This is a two-Act play based on the patriotic activities of the famous Indian nationalist leader Bal Gangadhar Tilak.

धन्योऽहं धन्योऽहम् Written by G.B. Palsule. A play with 4 Acts, (where the Acts are further subdivided into scenes) is based on the life of Vinayak Damodar Savaikar, popularly called Veer (Valiant) Savarkar (1883-

1966), the grand personality who was a hero of India's fight for freedom from the British thraldom.

म्याक्समूलारवैदुष्यम् by Bhavani Shankar Trivedi, 1981. A drama on the scholastic activities of the great Sanskrit scholar Maxmuller.

केशर-चङ्क्रमणम् by Shibaprasad Bhardwaj, Visva-Samskrtam, (J) 1963, Hosiarpur, Punjab, On Lala Lajpat Ray.

आयुरारोग्य-सौख्यम् by E. P. Bharata Pisharodi, Eranellur Trichur, Kerala 1 Ed, 1989.

The theme of the play is based on the eventful early period of the life of Melpathur Narayana Bhattapada, who according to the author was an extraordinary genius in the field of Sanskrit literature, especially in grammar and poetry, can hardly be compared with any poet or scholar of later centuries.

श्रीगीतगौराङ्गम् by Birendra Kumar Bhattacharyya, Calcutta – 1974. A lyrical play (*Gīti-naṭyam*) on the life and religion of Gaurāṅga Caitanya, the great preacher of selfless love towards both man and God.

सिद्धार्थचरितम् by Birendra Kumar Bhattacharyya, Calcutta – 1970. A drama in 8 acts, based on the life and positivistic Philosophy of Gautama Buddha, the great proponent of the doctrine of non-violence.

युगजीवनम् by Roma Chaudhuri (1967, Calcutta) on the life and teachings of Sri Ramakrishna. It is divided into ten scenes and has been staged all over India.

विवेकानन्दविजयम् by S. B. Varnekar, pubd. By Vivekananda Rock Memorial committee, Madras; 1972.

This is a homage to Vivekanada, by the author, in the form of a drama. In this drama (a *mahānaṭaka* in 10 Acts) a perfect synthesis of history and imagination is traceable. Exercising his imagination, the playwright brings out the spirit of the life-mission of the hero, the Hindu *sannyāsi* Vivekananda of International renown. Prof. Varnekar's poetic mind seems to be influenced to a great extent by Rama Krishna Vivekanada movement.

So far the technique & structure are concerned the drama is very much conventional since the type is of *mahānaṭaka* with 10 Acts, *Nāndī*, *Bhārata-vākya* are very much present. But innovation is found in absence of any Rasa as such.

Plays Based on Modern topics

"अत्रादिपदेन महाभारतादीतिहास लोकसमाजानां ग्रहणम् रामायणादिप्रसिद्धम्"[11]

"the word 'Aūṛs' includes the episodes of *Mahābhārata* etc.

and the contemporary issues of the societies as well"

This category appears to be most important of all. What is worth mentioning and which is inspiring at the same time is that the Sanskrit – scholars, like any other scholars in any field are also affected by the turmoil and vicissitudes of the pressing problems of the society. Verily, some sections of the Sanskrit scholars of present century still cling to the old, time – honoured theory of literary exercise; they cannot accommodate any deviation from their conservative outlook. But the exceptions are a large number of 20th/21st Century Sanskrit playwrights, short story writers and novelists. The Sanskrit scholars like all other social beings of the present century are also affected by the turmoils and the vicissitudes of pressing problems of the society. The trend of selecting themes from contemporary political, social, academic, industrial scenes and treatment thereof, either in serious veins or with sarcasm, is evident in their writings. The problems of modern India, socio-economic, political, psychological or so didn't lie beyond the range of the visions of Sanskrit litterateurs who normally are known for their bigotry and for clinging to the time-honoured theme, theory and technique. Thus, people, generally considered to be aloof from all the vicissitudes of socio-political tangles, too cannot but respond to society's call.

Thus the dramas are on 'Indo-China war', on 'Kashmir issue; on "Widow marriage' on 'child marriage', on 'Superstition' e. g. 'child-immolation' ect., on 'refugee influx, on 'Demoralization of society', 'System of Bureaucracy', 'communalism', 'Apartheid', and on many more issues in the context of present-day, social milieu deserve mention.

वेष्टनव्यायोगः is a playlet on Gherao written by Dr. B. K. Bhattacharyya of Bengal published at Calcutta in 1971 A. D. There cannot be a stronger satire on the policy of 'Gherao'. V. V. is characterized by fresh approach, novel thought and by modernity – in true sense of the term.

धारित्रीपतिनिर्वाचनम् (Stage performance – 1969) pubd. Calcutta, 1971. is an enjoyable satirical playlet, based on the contemporary political condition of the whole world, written by Dr. Siddhewar Chattopadhyay of Bengal. There cannot be any stronger attack or any pointed satire on contemporary political condition in international scenario. The International body known as UNO (United Nations Organization), the super powers with their huge arsenal of deadly weapons; the policy of non-alignment of neutral nations with their unjustified pride and many more aspects of contemporary political scene get lashes of sharp satire from the facile pen of the author.

अथ किम् is a Sanskrit playlet of Satirical type (*vyanga natika*) written by Dr. Siddheswar Chattopadhyay of Bengal (popularly known as *Buroda*) in 1969. (performed on stage – 1972, 2001)

Atha kim is a savoury Sanskrit playlet with a severe reproof towards our system of Democracy, towards all the political parties of Bengal rather India and especially towards our system 'Election'.

Herein no story as such is found. All the characters are introduced by mere symbols and not by individual names; since in each case the personal identity of the individual is not important, important is the 'class' or 'the political idea' they represent, Thus all the characters, representative of different classes etc, are introduced, interestingly enough with a peculiar combination of vowels and consonants e. g. 'Kaḥ' 'Khaḥ' etc.

ननाविताडनम् S. S. P. (J), Calcutta, vol LVII, 1974.

This is a savoury Sanskrit play of satirical type written by the same author of Bengal, based on the present humiliating condition of Sanskrit. There can't be any sharper satire on those 'elites' who being at the helm of academic affairs shed crocodile tears for the abolition of Sanskrit but inwardly endeavour for her abolition from all the academic curriculums in west Bengal.

मातृहननम्; जननीश्राद्धवासरम् Two playlets by Nityanada of Bengal; संस्कृतवाग्विजय: by Prabhudatta Shastri of Delhi are on the same theme of present condition of Sanskrit.

जननी is a modern one – act play written by Dr. Gouri Dharmapal (penname Uma Devisurya) in September 1984. The work is not yet published. 'Janani', with its lucid style, simple but dignified language, with occasional use of Bengali language, with its novel theme revealing the identity of 'Mother' – of the 'House Mother', or Sanskrit', of 'India' and of 'Mother soil' or 'Earth', bringing out the multi-lingual and the integrated aspect of India, depicting integration in its different aspects e.g., family integration, linguistic integration, national and East – West integration and with an ultimate objective of ushering into the traditional realm of peace, harmony, tolerance and integration will ever been enshrined in the hearts of the connoisseur.

तृणजातकम् (1983, 1st ed, Himachal pradesh). This is an I act play divided into a number of scenes written by Durgadatta Shastri of the Kangra district in Himachal pradesh. The drama showing how the usurer amasses wealth by taking advantage of the impoverished people who are generally subjected to extortion, exposing the harmful system of bonded labour highlighting the restriction connected with the caste-system etc. in a nutshell, the drama pointing out some darkest corners our socio-economic system in the present century deserves appreciation from all connoisseurs.

सोमप्रमम् (by Radhavallabh Tripathi) on the problem of dowry highlights crime against woman-folk. The play has been staged a number of times (1986 onwards).

यौतुकम् Varanassi, 1986 A.D. is an one-act play written by Shivaji Upadhyay of Uttar Pradesh. The play shows how the harmful system of 'dowry' still now prevalent in our modern society is oppressing the father who is burdened with a marriageable daughter for whom marriage can't be settled without a huge amount of dowry for the bridegroom. The style is lucid, language is simple and the topic is modern and relevant to this present day society. Our author says sarcastically – *Yautakaṃ nanu sarvasvam yautakaṃ mānamūlakam, yautakam kanyakā sūlam yautakam varamulyakam* and draws our attention to this problem of our society.

दरिद्र-दुर्दैवम् Calcutta, 1968. by Srijiva Nyayatirtha of Bengal on demoralization of present day society.

हकीकतरायनाटकम् by Hazarilal Sharma of Haryana on 'Communalism'.

In all the above mentioned Dramas, 'Innovation'plays a major role compared to tradition. For that reason, all the mentioned dramas have been encompassed as representative ones.

It will not be out of place to mention here that the plays based on contemporary political issue e. g. on Kashmir problem or on U.N.O. which throw some sarcastic flings are included in this category and not in the first category.

Plays based on the episodes of Upanisads/ Puranas/ Ramayana / Mahabharata

"ख्यातं रामायणादिप्रसिद्धम्"12

'ख्यात' means some well-known fact from the *Rāmāyaṇa* etc.

From time immemorial Ramayana, Mahabharata, Puranas etc. are the eternal source of continuous flow of themes and ideas that are woven into literary creations. Quite obviously the dramas based on Puranas etc are huge in number.

गुप्तपाशुपतम् Bombay, 1975. by Viswanath Satyanarayan of Andhra Pradesh based on the episode of Mahabharata gives a new interpretation of the great Kurukṣetra war.

नर्तनशाला Bombay, 1983 by Ogeti Parikṣit Sharma of Andhra Pradesh, based on the *Kicakavadha* episode of the vanaparva of Mahābhārata.

श्रवणम् by the same author is based on the familiar episode of Daśaratha's life (i.e., killing of the blind sage by Dauaratha) traceable in the *Rāmāyaṇa*.

एकचक्रम् Bangalore, 1990. by N. Ranganatha Sharma of Karnataka deals with the episode of Kunti and *Pañca Pāndava* found in the Mahabharata.

शौरिशौर्यम् By Jaggu Singaracharya deals with Krishna's exploits in boyhood traceable in *Vishnu Purana* and *Bhagavat Purana*. The playwright has remodelled the Puranic theme with a few remarkable innovations.

महीयसी गार्गी Calcutta, 1976 A.D. by Brahmacarini Bela Devi, of Bengal is based on the story of *Bṛhadāraṇyakopaniṣad*.

नचिकेतश्चरितम् Calcutta, 1976 A.D., by the same authoress of Bengal is based on the wonderful story of Naciketa found in *Kathopaniṣad*. In all the works of Bela Devi to restate the lofty ideas of ancient India preached by Vedas, *Upaniṣads* etc. seems to be the primary aim of the authoress who herself was associated with some religious institutions.

प्रायोपवेशनम् Howrah, West Bengal, 1972 A.D. by Pandit Durgaprasanna Vidyabhusansa of Bengal is based on the episode found in the *Vanaparvan* of the *MBH*. (the episode of the sage Durvasas and his disciples).

एकलव्य-गुरुदक्षिणम् Calcutta, 1971 A.D. by the same author is based on the tragic Ekalavya episode found in the *Ādiparvan* of the MBH.

आत्मनिवेदनम् by(staged 2008) by Shanti Nath Ghosh based on the same theme. New interpretation is appreciable.

माणवक-गौरवम् Calcutta, 1958. by Mm. Kalipada Tarkacarya is an elegant play with seven acts based on the story of MBH concerning the great sage and the teacher Dhaumya and his disciples.

In all the above mentioned dramas tradition plays a major role regarding theme, but innovation is noticeably found in the reinterpretation of the themes.

Let the case of the last drama be considered. Apparently the playwright predominantly belongs to the old tradition since he follows the technique and the style of the traditional dramatists; he uses *nandi*, *bharatavakya*, *sandhis*, etc. in a most conventional way, but the drama primarily aims at the glorification of '*gurubhakti*' i.e., the devotion to a teacher, which is an essentiality for student community, without which a student can not ever succeed. A character personifying the abstract quality e.g., *Gurubhakti* and a number of gnomic verses are inserted for the glorification of the said quality – an essential virtue which is lacking in the modern age.

Play Based on Quasi-Historical-Episodes / Legends / Anecdotes

"दृष्टपूर्वा अपि ह्यर्थाः
काव्ये रसपरिग्रहात् ।
सर्वे नवा इवाभान्ति
मधुमास इव द्रुमाः"13॥

A novel and appreciable trend is very much prominent among the Sanskrit dramatists of twentieth century A.D. to reconstruct the lives and personalities of the great poets and poetesses through the form of a drama. In most of the cases they have based their themes on the anecdotes or legends centred around the lives of some celebrated figures e.g., Valmiki, Kalidasa. Sometimes the authors have created the plays from the minimum of the matter with them e.g., a few verses found in the anthologies or quoted in some other Sanskrit texts. In this category we've found near about twenty-five dramas. Some of them are enumerated below.

भासोऽहासः Pune, 1980. this is a non-pareil play, written by Prof. G.B. Palsule of Maharashtra with three acts where the acts are again subdivided into screnes. This plot is completely imaginary but still centres round the traditional story of burning of all the dramas (except *Svapnavasavadattam*) of Bhasa by the judges recorded in the famous lines – Bhasa – *nāṭakacakre'pi chekaikṣipte parīkṣitum* etc.

Dr. Palsule, the author of this drama has successfully and strikingly enough tried to give a splendidly rational interpretation viz., the society did not tolerate that the playwright should not be faithful to the sacred writings of Vyasa and Valmiki; or the society would not tolerate the poet like Bhasa (the hero of this drama) who should have made heroes out of villains.

अनारकलि Madras, 1972. is a ten act play written by Prof. V. Raghavan of Madras based on some well known quasi-historical romantic episode connected with the secret love between Salim (later on emperor Jahangir) and Anarkali-immaculately beautiful lady (attendant) in the Mughal harem. The play is a great step for national integration. It projects an overall ideology of integration and harmony.

आदिकविः Bharati (J), Bihar by Buddhadev Pandeya of Bihar on the life of Kalidasa.

कालिदासचरितम् Maharashtra, 1961. by S.B. Velankar on the life of Kalidasa.

प्रेक्षणकत्रयी By Dr. V. Raghavan of Tamil Nadu, based on the lives of three famous poetesses of India. Vijayanka, Vikatanitamtamba, and Avantisundari.

प्रेमपीयुषम् By R.V. Tripathi of Madhyapradesh on the qausi-historical incidents connected with the life of the poet Bhavabhuti.

भर्तृहरीयम् By V.D. Gangal of Maharashtra on the life of Bhartihari based on the famous Verse of Nitisataka *"dhik tam ca tām ca"*.

दस्युरत्नाकरम् By Visvervara Vidyabhusana Manjusa (J) 1957.

आदिकवेरुदभवम् By Jayashri Nag, Burdwan, W.B., 1984 A.D.

प्रशान्तरत्नाकरम् By Kalipada Tarkacarya [S.S.P.P. (J) Calcutta, 1938-39]

All the Three are based more or less on the theme of how bandit Ratnakar was transformed into Valmiki – the great poet of Rāmāyaia.

Thus in this category also tradition plays a major role i.e., tradition is followed regarding structure but as regards theme and spirit 'innovation' is conspicuously traceable in almost all the dramas.

Plays Adapted/Translated form other languages

Translations are esteemed to be as important as the creative works, since they fulfil a double purpose, viz., the works in the Sanskrit language are enriched in one hand on the other these are helpful to understand the literary values of the original creations in other languages especially the vernacular ones and thereby contribute to national integrity. दीनार्किराजकुमारहेमलेखम् This is a Sanskrit version of William Shakespeare's 'Hamlet' by Dr. Sukhamoy Mukherjee. Published at Delhi in 1971 A. D. The Hamlet has been acclaimed as the greatest among the tragedics of Shakespeare. Moreover, it is esteemed as the most popular as well as most problematical play ever written. The original 'Hamlet' is indeed noted for abundance of such quotable apophthegms. Our translator's successful renderings of such passages deserve special attention and acclaim here. The advice of Polonius to his son Laertes, Hamlet's observations on man in Act II before Rosencrantz and Guildenstern and of course the famous and profound "To be or not to be" of Hamlet are worth-mentioning here.

चन्द्रसेनः is another outstanding translation of Hamlet by S. D. Joshi & Vighnahari Deo of Pune (Maharashtra); (यूथिका, 1976) is the translation of famous Romeo-Juliet of Shakespeare by Revaprasad Dwivedi of

Madhyapradesh. Besides, a number of translations are made in dramatic form from vernaculars e.g., Marathi, Telugu, Bengali. More than '20' of Tagore's dramas / short stories have been translated in the form of drama. Of which वाल्मीकिप्रतिभा (New Delhi, 1966) by V. Raghavan of Madras, रथरज्जुः (S. S P (J), 43rd yr Nos 8-12) by Dr. Bimal Krishna Matilal of Bengal; मुक्तधारा, वार्तागृहम् (Calcutta, 1963) by Dr. Dhyanesh Narayan Chakravorty of Bengal, सम्पत्तिसमर्पणम् (Howrah (W.B.) 1978) and गुप्तधनम् (Howrah, W.B., 1987) by Pandit Nityananda Smititirtha of Bengal deserve special attention.

Muktadhara, the greatest of Tagore's symbolical play and *Dakghar* – a gentle and deeply moving play in Bengali have successfully and elegantly been translated by Dhyanesh Narayan Chakrabarti being titled as *Muktadhara* and *Vartagriham* respectively.

However in consideration of lucidity and simplicity, application of selected sounds, these productions are indeed joy for ever to Tagore-lovers and Sanskrit-lovers as well. It seems all of them have proved the inappropriateness of the saying –

"The perfume of a pristine thought
Can't in translation be caught"

By way of specimen, mention may be made about the following. In the first Act after the exit of the curd-seller, Amal says (in toning) *"Curds, Curds, Curds from the country of the panchmura hills by the Shyamli bank, curds, good curds. In the early morning the women make the cows stand in a row under the trees and milk them and in the evening, they turn the milk into curds, good curds»*, etc.

Where Tagore says *"dai, dai, bhalodai, sei pancmuda pahader talay samli nadir dhare gaylader barir dai. Tara bhorer velai gacher talay goru damd kariye dudh doy. sadhyavelay meyera dai pate sei dai"*.

And Dhyaneshnarayana almost in the same tone and spirit says – *(Gitasvarena) dadhi, dadhi, uttamamdadhi, tadhi pancacudasaila-tate*

*syamalinadi tiravartighosangananam dadhi, te hi prabhatakale – –
dadhi, dadhi-da-a-dhi, uttamam dadhi* etc.

Those, in the readers, who don't know Bengali, they even can note amazing and startling resemblance between the two versions-the Bengali (original) and its translation in Sanskrit. In this category, there is no scope as such to point out the synthesis of tradition & innovation. Because a good translator has little scope to show his innovative acumen.

Plays on miscellaneous topics

There are a large number of dramas which are found to be difficult to place within the periphery of any particular category as such because almost each and every of them is a category by itself. So it seems to be appropriate to club all those together in this category, which may be termed as 'Miscellaneous'. In this category a sharp departure from traditional track is found and naturally innovation plays a major role. However, due to paucity of space no play is introduced in this category.

From the above discussion it may safely be surmised that a sharp deviation form the orthodox point of view is conspicuously observed in the Sanskrit plays of the Post Independence period. This deviation is traceable in the short-stories and other genres too.

In the plays mentioned above in Category I we observe, primarily, the extra ordinary heroic activities of Rana Pratap Singh of Mewar; the exploits of the great Maratha King Shivaji; theme relating to Chandragupta Maurya and Chanakya – an amulgum of history and myth, so to say, evoked equal interest in modern days also, as we may gather from the composition of a number of plays, introduced in our paper. The basic intension of the dramatist appears to be to revive the past glory of India. Some plays in this category are based either on the incidents connected with the Freedom Movement of India e.g. Satyagraha movement, Civil Disobedience movement, Daṇḍi yatra, etc. or on the lives and the patriotic activities of the Freedom fighters e.g.,

Veer Savarkar, Bal Gangadhar Tilak, Jatindra Nath Mukherjee, Netaji Subhas Ch. Bose, Chittranjan Das and so on.

In the plays under category-II we find internationally significant religious and spiritual figures like Shankaracharya, Ramkrishna Paramahaósa, Swami Vivekananda; political personalities e.g. Mahatma Gandhi, Pandit Jawaharlal Nehru, Dr. Bidhan Chandra Roy, Churchill and so on; popular saints, mystics and devotees e.g., Jñāneśvara Ramdas, Tukaram, Mirabai; renowned scholars e.g. MaxMuller, Rabindranath Tagore have become the subject of biographical plays.

The most interesting and notable feature is that these biographical plays centred round some renowned personalities are necessarily novel departure from the convention so far 'Rasa' is concerned. Actually, any particular Rasa-Vīra or Śṛṅgāra, which, according to tradition is the very primary criterion of a náôaka, is not traceable here but the aesthetic success of most of the plays can't be denied.

Category-III proves how the Sanskrit scholars, like any other scholars in any field are also affected by the turmoil's and changes of the society. In category III, it is observed that all the modern problems may it be social, political or economic, may it be socio-political, socio religious or socio-economic, didn't lie beyond the range of the visions of Sanskrit dramatist who normally are considered to be aloof from all the present social milieu. Thus play on 'dowry', on 'Gherao', on 'refugee influx, on Naxalite movement', on 'problems of Industrial workers' 'decadence in morality', on 'decadence in democracy', on 'System of Parliamentary Election', on 'Indiscipline and ideological problem among the students, on 'System of education', on 'Corruption in politics', on 'pitiable condition of Indian Women and widows', on 'Family planning', on 'Apartheid', on 'multilingual problem', on 'problem of working lady', on 'problem of Khalistan', on 'unemployment issue', on 'drug abuse', on 'Leprosy', on 'child-marriage', on 'National integration', and on many more contemporary issues are composed especially in the post-Independence period.

The plays from Category III and from IV-are chosen for detailed discussion simply because they undoubtedly do have some significant contribution exclusively from sociological standpoint.

Technique

> *"The phrase Alienation Effect (A-Effect in short) has become very popular in the realm of our modern theatre"*

Adaptation to modern dramatic technique in the Sanskrit plays of the post-Independence period is also a remarkable event in this context.

As found in Western plays the acts are generally divided into scenes. Occasionally there is no act-division, the play is divided into a number of scenes. For instance, – '*Kā vārtā Mādhuryam*' etc. published in *Navamālati* (New Delhi 1997) composed by Nodanatha Mishra may be mentioned. A number of other plays also may be named as the cases in point.

The essential gorgeous forms of the stages are transformed into simplified forms due to progressive outlook of the playwrights. The influence of group-theatre plays and of Marxist dramas especially of E.F. Brecht can't be denied. Sometimes the characters acting some roles play the part of some inanimate objects. The play '*Maśakaddhānī*' by R. V. Tripathi in which four persons act as four stands of a mosquito-net, may be cited as the most relevant example here. The play has been performed on stage a number of times in 1995, 96 and successive years).

During current times the orthodox concept of a firm barrier between the stage and the spectators has been removed giving a new dimension to the dramatic technique. Occasionally, the characters performing on the stage are seen to come out from the spectators underlining the inseparable identity between the characters performing on the stage and the characters watching as spectators. Thus in the play '*Ganeśapūjanam*' five or six persons from the first row of the audience act as the characters of the play; in *Nanāvitādanam* by Siddheswar Chattopadhyaya person from audience comes on the stage and act as an actor. Abstract plays, Radio – plays (*Nabho-nātya* or *Śruti-nātya*), symbolic plays, operas or *Gītinātyas*, street – plays are produced. One – act plays infringing the dramaturgical conventions *Pañcādika* are being produced and performed in a considerable number keeping in pace with the fast life of the modern age. The introduction of 'Flashback' system in Sanskrit plays is a noticeable feature indeed. At times, all the characters, especially in the Abstract plays, are introduced by mere symbols and not by individual names since in each case the personal identity of the individual is not important, important is the 'class' or the idea' they represent. Thus interestingly enough in '*Atha kim*' by Siddheswar Chattopadhyaya of Bengal all the characters, representative of different classes etc, are introduced with a peculiar combination of vowels, consonants and spirant (visarga). For instance, therein '*kaḥ*' represents the educated middle-class people who have lost all interests in politics and can't be swayed easily by political propaganda of the political party-leaders, '*khaḥ*' represents the lower middle-class people who are hard-pressed and are finding it quite difficult to meet all the basic necessities in present socio-economic and sociopolitical situation of India; '*gaḥ*', '*ghaḥ*', *ṅaḥ*' etc. represent spokesmen of different political parties of India.

In this context the plays published in '*Mṛtyu*' etc., by Harshdev Madhav may be mentioned with special emphasis. The influence of 'third theatre' as publicized by the noted director and thespian Shri Badal Sarkar of West Bengal can conspicuously be observed in Harshdev's plays. All the plays are either 'abstract' or 'symbolic' in character. The play '*Kabrasthāne*', through the conversation of two spirits exposes sarcastically the hollowness of human life.

In the play titled '*Kāmalā*' the deadly disease 'jaundice' has been depicted to symbolize all pervading decadence in presentday society. In almost all his plays, the playwright shows how human beings are drifting along aimlessly everlost in the labyrinth of mundane needs and worries. All of Harshdev's plays bearing symbolic and significant titles; having high doses of histrionic element are undoubtedly outstanding departure from the conventional track. Though the playwright has tried to present some plays as surprising stunts, yet whether they are all that praiseworthy or not leaves work for the connoisseur.

Besides, a number of dramas of the said period do not belong to the same traditional pattern. For instance, there are modern plays in Sanskrit which are neither '*sutradhāra-kṛtārambha*' nor divided into '*aṅka*' etc; neither they begin with conventional '*nāndī*' nor do they end with '*bharatavākya*'. There is no '*nandœ* in a good many number of plays e.g., **Nanāvitāḍanam, Kā vārtā, Mādhuryam, Raktābhiṣekam** etc. In some places, ' *nāndī* 's are there, but conventional deities e. g. Vioiu, Uiva, and so on are not invoked. So in the play "*Uttiṣṭha Kaunteya*", '*Śrīmagbhagavadgītā*" has been worshipped; ' *nāndī'* of "*Svapnājjāgaraṇam varam*", invokes God of dream! At places, ' *nāndī*' are there but in unconventional form. The *nāndī* of the play '**Dārāśikohīyam**' where our country, India speaks about herself roughly in the form of an autobiography may be cited as a wonderful instance.

There are plays ending without '*bharatavākyas*'; moreover there are plays ending with conventional '*bharatavākyas*' but in unconventional form. ***Cakrānusaraṇam Dārāśikohiyam Badhū-dahanam Dveṣadamśanam Veṣṭana-vyāyogaḥ, Raktābhiṣekam*** may be mentioned as relevant pieces here.

Different songs are inserted in the plays. Each and every one has got its distinctive flavour strikingly but exclusively of its own. Most of the songs have got some unstrained and spontaneous appeal. The songs of the labourers eulogizing *Veṣṭana* or *Gherao* 'the sarcastic song in the Gazal' song in *Navamālatī* (p. 72), the chorus song of the common people depicting decadence in democracy and exposing Bofors scam (Pañca-parṇam, P.2) and many more are extremely suitable to their respective situations. '*Kirtan*' style in the song of *Nanāvitaḍanam*, '*Bhajan*' and pop song in '*Dhanam*' deserve special mention in this context. The modern playwrights in general are found to be very much careful about the background music. They clearly indicate the specific tone of the music reflecting the mood of the situation. As such happy (*prasannatā dyotakam kṣipram – samgītam-Sapta* – P 112), or melancholic (*avasādasamgītam – Sapta* – P.112), light or serious (*gambhīra dhvani, Sapta* – P.174) moods are reflected through the background music. Besides different sounds e. g. the typical sound of the taking off and landing of the air-crafts; (*vimānāgama dhvanih, vimāna-prasthāna-dhvaniḥ* etc. Sapta – P. 135, 138, 140), of the chanting of Vedic hymns (Sapta – P-145), twittering of the harbingers of dawn (*Sapta* – P.144) and many more effect – music are distinctly indicated by the playwrights to make the performance of the plays easier and more enjoyable too.

Thus we find as with the themes, so also with the dramatic technique, a perfect blend of tradition and innovation is conspicuously found in Sanskrit plays of the Post Independence period.

Language

"सर्वेषां कारणवशात्

कार्यः भाषाव्यतिक्रमः"

As with the themes, so also with the literary idioms, a perfect blend of tradition and innovation in the terms of coined words, allusion, popular maxims and the like brings forth a new mode of stylistics of figurative language.

Prākṛit, the conventional language for *cetī, vidūṣaka* and the like is omitted in almost all the plays under discussion probably to make the understanding of the general viewers easier. Sometimes vernaculars e.g., Bengali Punjabi, Oriya etc., and Hindi are used.

Occasionally words, idioms or popular maxims from English language and Persian too are used comfortably instead of Prākṛit or vernaculars.

Performance

"दृश्यं तत्राभिनेयम्"

"The play is for representation"

It goes without saying that whenever a playwright writes or a director (*Sūtradhāra*) plans a play, he arranges the incidents of the plot in such a way that those can be presented and performed by the actors and actresses of his own time. The playwright or the Director (*Sūtradhāra*) always keeps in his mind the contemporary mode of representation and stage convention. Sanskrit play is no exception to this general rule of evolution as revealed in the history of theatre and drama.

Bharata's *Nāṭyaśāstra* mentions the title of two plays: – 'Amṛtamanthana' and 'Tripuradāha' – which were performed during the period of composition and compilation of *Nāṭyaśāstra*; which gives detailed account of stage, stage-craft, mode of representation, stage convention, spectators, theatre-hall, gestures, movements and so on and so forth. It may safely be stated, that the plays of Kālidāsa, Bhavabhūti, Viśākhadatta, Bhaooanarayaia, Uraeharoa and others were certainly composed for representation. Unfortunately no written records have come down to us to give an idea of the stage etc. of that period.

Coming to the 20th/21st century hearing about enactment of Sanskrit plays might be a bit of surprise for many of us. But even today such Sanskrit plays; – both classical and modern are being produced on stage though not on a very large scale.

In the post-Independence period a number of Sanskrit plays (original/ translated /adapted) were staged by a number of organizations e.g., 'Prācyāvaṇi', Calcutta; Sanskrit Sahitya Parishat, Calcutta; Howrah Sanskrit Sahitya Samaj, Surabharati Sanskrit Insititute, Kolkata; Sopanam, Kerala; 'Arghya' Kolkata and by a number of individual Sanskrit lovers and Theatre-lovers e.g., J.B. Chaudhuri, Roma Chaudhuri, B.K. Bhattacharyya, Nityananda Smititirtha, Dhyanesh Narayan Chakravorty, K.N. Panikkar, Siddheswar Chattopadhyay, Haridasa Siddhanta Vāgæùa, Kalipada Tarkacharya, Rajendra Mishra, Rama Kanta Shukla, Radhavallabh Tripathi, Haridutt Sharma, Srijiva Nyayatirtha, G.B. Palsule, S.B. Varnekar, Siddheswar Chattopadhyay, Manish Mitra, and last but not the least Shantinath Ghosh.

Much more still needs to be said about Modern Sanskrit Plays of India. Through this present paper, primarily it has been tried to point out different novel trends, which are distinctly traceable in the compositions of Sanskrit playwrights. Some of them observed the traditional rules of dramaturgy to some extent and introduce certain experiments in theme, technique and spirit as well. A large number of playwrights have selected the themes of their plays from contemporary social, political, academic and industrial scenes occasionally with sarcastic fling towards the society and the individual as well. In most cases modern dramatists have ventured with the ultimate optimistic objective of ushering in a better society – full of peace and harmony. Another appreciable trend most conspicuously found in modern dramas is the trend of projecting the ethical values through the well-known episodes of *Upaniṣads*, *Rāmāyaṇa*, *Mahābhārata* and *Purāṇas* or re-interpreting the old theme with a specific objective. Besides, the trend to translate or to adapt from the works of great literary artists e. g. Shakespeare, Kālidāsa; Rabindranath Tagore; Bankim Chandra and many more and thereby to project the philosophy of those artists as reflected in the original – is very much prominent in the works of the dramatists of the present century. And to reproduce the great lives of the great souls of India in order to inspire the present generation is another noteworthy trend found in the modern dramas.

Sometimes the themes are traditional and innovation is found in the formation of structure and application of technique; in some cases the technique is traditional and innovation is found in selection and reinterpretation of theme; and in the rest cases 'innovation' perfectly overrules 'tradition'.

Thus there are Sanskrit Plays produced in the post-Independence period, which prove conclusively the high potentiality of the language and establish positively that even modern rather ultra-modern thoughts and incidents can be easily and wonderfully expressed in Sanskrit language.

The present authoress has carefully chosen a good many numbers of plays produced in different parts of this vast peninsula exclusively in the post-independence period to highlight the deviations and innovations mentioned above. She has made a humble attempt to establish the fact that though Sanskrit had lost its honourable status yet undoubtedly it continues to be to some extent a potential vehicle of thought and emotion. Above all, she has tried to draw the attention of the academic elites towards the commendable juxtaposition of 'tradition and innovation', 'tradition and modernity' which is conspicuously found in Modern Sanskrit plays of India.

So far the linguistic aspect is concerned how far such innovativeness or novel ventures will be acceptable to purists may be a question yet it must be remembered that it is an attempt to modernize Sanskrit and absorb a large number of words and literary idioms form the present day spoken languages so that Sanskrit, as the Sanskrit litterateurs earnestly desire "may have a footing in the practical life of the people".

But it is a matter of great regret that good many Bengali rather Indian prodigies – in the vast domain of modern Sanskrit Literature, with their outstanding contributions not only in *dṛśyakāvya* or drama section but in other fields too, – are passing into oblovion.

As a devoted lover of Sanskrit the present authoress will consider her humble effort amply rewarded if she has been able to draw attention of the connoisseurs towards the not-so-well-known talents of Modern India.

The more she goes deep into the subject the more is her feeling of not being able to project the different facets of the treasure up to her satisfaction. She is very much aware that there is much more scope of work in this vast area of Modern Sanskrit Literature where she has ventured to tread on.

"आ परितोषाद्विदुषां न साधु मन्ये प्रयोगविज्ञानम्"

"Unless and until the connoisseurs are satisfied I don't consider my venture successful"

Notes:

1. दशरूपक literally means 10 types of Rūpakas. In this paper Rūpaka/Nāṭaka is used as drama in general.

2. सन्दर्भेषु दशरूपकं श्रेयः – (Kāvyālamkarasūtravṛtti-1.3)

3. योऽयं स्वभावो लोकस्य सुखदुःखसमन्वितः सोहङ्गाद्यभिनयोपेतः-नाट्यमित्यभिधीयते। – Nāṭyaśāstra (GOS) – 1.119

4. दृश्यश्रव्यत्वभेदेन पुनः काव्यं द्विधामतम् Sāhitya VI

5. दृश्यं तत्राभिनेयम् – Sāhityadarpaṇa-VI

6. श्रव्यं श्रोतव्यमात्रम् – ibid Vi

7. 7a. न हि रसादृते कश्चिदप्यर्थः प्रवर्तते – Nāṭyaśāstra (GOS), VI

   7b. वाक्यं रसात्मकं काव्यम् Sāhityadarpaṇa – I

8. Mainly *Nāṭakas, Prakaraṇas* and *Prahasanas*. Other types are found in a meagre number.

9. In the definition of *Mahākāvya* it is stated by *Daṇḍin* that a Mahākāvya should be based on itihasa i.e., Rāmāyaṇa or Mahābhārata or on some great leader or on true facts. (Kāvyadarśa – 1)

   Kusumapratima commentary (on Sāhitya-Darpaṇa) by Mm. Haridāsa Siddhāntavāgīśa. "The word *ādī* includes everything whatever or whoever is well-known through Mahābhārata, history; purāṇa or in contemporary society.

10. Sāhitya-Darpaṇa – VI

11. *ibid*-VI (from the commentary of Mm. Haridāsa Siddhāntavāgīśa)

12. *ibid*-VI

13. Dhvanyāloka

[*Note* – This paper was published in *Arghya Journal* 2009 Issue-1 (Theatre Organ of Kasba Arghya), Page – 20]

6

Saiṣā Sarvaiva Vakroktiḥ

From the Vedas to Modern Bengali Literature

Thomas Gray (1716-1771), the famous English poet who was considered to be a precursor of Romanticism, wrote in one of his letters – *"Our poetry has a language peculiar to itself.»*[1] Alexander Bari (1818-1903), the noted European scholar said in the early 19th century *"A figure of speech is a deviation from the plain and ordinary mode of speaking for the sake of greater effect; it is an unusual form of speech.»*[2]

What the scholars like Alexander Bari or Thomas Gray have observed regarding the language of the poetry or what the famous French symbolist poet, philosopher and mathematician Paul Amboise Valery (1871-1945) observed as *"A language within a language"* in 18th century A.D. has already been given a finished form, explicitly explained. and firmly established as a unique theory of *Vakrokti* by Kuntaka in his legendary work *'Vakrokti-Jivitam'* way back in 10th century A.D.

Now by whatever name we may call *Vakrokti*, name it a 'figurative expression', or an 'artistic utterance', or a poetic, or an 'ornamental', or an 'extraordinary expression', no poet or poeticist could avoid its existence whatsoever.

The etymological meaning of the term *Vakrokti* is 'crooked speech' or 'arch speech' and this meaning appears in the verbal poetic figure defined[3] by Rudrata.

In Vamana, *Vakrokti* does not mean a verbal figure. It is defined[4] as a metaphorical mode of speech based on 'lakṣanā i.e. transference of sense.

By *Vakrokti* some theorists of Dhvani school, Rasa school etc. connote a kind of pretended speech based on paronomasia (śleṣa) or peculiarities of intonation (kāku). Viśvanātha in his 'Sāhitya-Darpaṇa' says

anyasyānyārthakaṃ vākyamanyathā yojayed yadi.
anyo śleṣeṇa kākvā vā sā vakroktistato dvidhā//-X/II

It will not be out of place to mention here, we would not take into account the connotation of *Vakrokti* as desired by Vāmana or Viśvanātha but we would accept the connotation as defined by Bhāmaha and later on developed by Kuntaka.

However Dandin in his Kavyadarsa divides this literary world into two broad divisions:

bhinnaṃ dvidhā svabhāvoktirvakroktiśceti vāṅmayam/[5]-II/363
Rajasekhara in his Kavya-mimamsā adds one more variety and says
vakroktiśca rasoktiśca svabhāvoktiśceti vāṅmayam-V/8

The following remark of the poet Manoratha belonging to Anti-dhvani school-

yasminnasti na vastu kiñcana manaḥ prahlādi sālamkriti
vyutpannai racitam ca naiva vacanair vakroktisunyam ca yat/
kāvyam tad dhvaninā samanvitamiti ...etc.

shows that during his time the concept of Vakrokti, if not in the form of theory, was already in the place and was well accepted to the world of scholars.

Mahimabhatta is more clear in putting forward-

prasiddham margamutsrjya yatra vaicitryasiddhaye
anyathaivocyate so'rtha sā vakrokti-rudahṛtā /

which seems to be translated as it were by J. Mukarovsky of "Prague School of Poetic Division" who says in unequivocal terms:[6]

Poetic language is a different form of language with a different function from that of the standard.

Thus Vakrokti as understood by Bhamaha and his followers seems to be echoed in the saying of Bhojadeva who says in the first chapter of his Srngaraprakasa in unambiguous terms,

yadavakram vacaḥ śāstre loke ca vaca eva tat
vakram yadarthavādādau tasya kavyamiti sthitam//

The famous commentator Samudrabandha in course of commenting upon Ruyyaka's '*Alaṃkārsarvasvam*' has compiled five major established theories as related to 'Word' and 'Meaning' and has included Vakrokti-theory as one of them. Therein Samudrabandha explains *Vakrokti as bhaṇiti-vaicitrya.*

Srīharṣa in his Naiṣadhacaritam appreciates *Vakrokti*[7] as revealed in the speech of his accomplished heroine Damayanti.

In Jayadeva's Gītagovindam, we find Srikrishna remembers other qualities of Radha along with her *'girāṃ vakrimā'* and becomes enthralled.

According to Bhamaha, the founder of *Alaṃkara* school, Vakrokti is the cahracter or essence of poetry. In Bhamaha we find certain *alaṃkaras* were not regarded as *alaṃkaras* as there was no Vakrokti in them. There Bhamaha says

saisā sarvaiva vakroktir anayārtho vibhāvyate
yatno 'syāṃ kavinā kāryaḥ ko 'lankāro 'nayā vinā//Bhā – II/85[8]

Vakrokti as the soul of poetry is therefore not a discovery or invention of Kuntaka but it was he who gave it a finished form. By *Vakrokti* Bhamaha meant poetic or artistic expression other than ordinary or naturalistic expression, that is all adorned or ornamental expression[9][10] as abhorrent to matter-of-fact speech. Vakrokti, said Bhāmaha, was the means by which the meaning was rendered delightful; in short *Vakrokti* flashes 'Rasa'. 'Rasa' therefore, is subordinate to *Alaṃkara* and *Alaṃkara* is founded on *Vakrokti*. Abhinavagupta makes this clear in his Locana commentary saying *...sabdasya hi vakratā...*etc.

However the idea of *Vakrokti* was carried to an extreme by Kuntaka and his *Vakrokti-jīvitam* enunciates the theory that Vakrokti is life of poetry and that comprehends in it other caharacteristics of poetry like *Alaṅkāra, Dhvani* etc.

Kuntaka defines 'Vakrokti'

Ubhavetāvalaṃkāryau tayoḥ punaralamkṛtiḥ
Vakroktireva vaidagdhya-bhangī-bhaṇitirucyate /

According to Kuntaka, both words and meanings deserve to be looked upon as the subjects of ornamentation for the enhancement of their appeal. One might ask – "*what then is their ornament?*" The answer is that '*though they are two in number they have only one common ornament-and that is Vakrokti.*'

Kuntaka, who developed the idea of Bhāmaha's Vakrokti, and builds a unique theory of poetics on its basis, makes the meaning clear when he says in his vrtti-

vakroktiḥ prasiddhābhidhāna-vyatirekiṇī vicitraivābhidhā. kīdṛśī
vaidagdhya-bhaṅgibhaṇiti[11] vaidagdhyaṃ vidagdha-bhāvaḥ
kavikarmakausalam tasya bhaṅgī vicchittiḥ, tasya bhaṇitiḥ
vicitraivabhidhā vakrokti rityucyate/[12]

So by such '*vakratā*', the peculiar charm (*vicchitti*) or strikingness (*vaicitrya*) can be imparted to ordinary i.e. matter-of-fact expression by the conception of the poet.

Thus when the words are used in the ordinary manner of common parlance, by the poeple without a poetic turn of mind, there is no special charm or '*vichitti*' no strikingness or '*vaicitrya*' and consequently it is not poetical in the sense in which Bhamaha or Kuntaka understands it.

Kuntaka defines 'kāvya'-

śabdārthau sahitau vakra-kavi-vyāpāraśālini
bandhe vyavasthitau kāvyaṃ tadvidhāhlādakāriṇi//[13]

'Word' and 'sense', the 'denoter' and 'denoted' taken together constitute poetry. In a good poetry word and sense enshrined in a style that reveals the artistic (lit. 'out of the way') creativity of the creator-poet i.e. *kavisraṣṭā* on one hand and gives aesthetic delight to the man of taste (*sahṛdaya*) on the other.

Now this *Vakratā* according to Kuntaka may be divided into six categories. Each one of them may have numerous subdivisions and all the subdivisions are characterised by striking shades of beauty. Six categories are as follows:

1. varṇavinyāsa – vakratā
2. padapūrvardha – vakratā
3. pratyaya – vakratā
4. vākya – vakratā
5. prakaraṇa-vakratā
6. prabandha – vakratā

of which *varṇavinyāsa-vakrata* an upacāra-vakratā, a subdivision of scecond category i.e. padapurvārdha-vakratā are our present concern.

According to Kuntaka one, two or more syllables used again and again at short intervals constitute the three forms[14] of varṇavinyāsa-vakratā i.e. "the art in the arrangement of syllables". Here '*varṇa*' stands for '*vyanjana varṇa*'[15] there are other cases of *varṇa-vinyasa-vakratā* which are thus clarified by Kuntaka as *varṇānta-yoginaḥ*.[16] ...which means consonants classified (*sparśavarṇa*) if combined with their nasals in alliteration; ta,la, na; may be doubled or reiterated; or the consonants might become conjunct with 'ra' in alliteration – all will shine by their harmony with the theme, all are the examples of *varṇa-vinyāsa-vakratā*. Now it is clear that all the cases of *anuprāsa* and *yamaka* come under this category of *vakratā*.

1. *pūrṇamadaḥ pūrṇamidaṃ pūrṇāt pūrṇamudacyate*
   pūrṇasya pūrṇamādāya pūrṇamevāvaśiṣyate //[17]
2. *vaśi sarvasya lokasya sthāvarasya carasya ca /*
3. *tāḍakā cala kapālakuṇḍalā /*
   kālikevā niviḍā valākinī//[18]
4. *khe khelagami tamuvāha vāhaḥ*[19]
5. *nava-palāśa-palāśa-vanaṃ puraḥ...*[20]
6. *prapañcaya pañcamaṃ vimuñca na muñca mām*[21]

Thus repetition of consonants exhibiting highest level of *varṇa-vinyāsa-vakratā* are traceable in Upanishadic text and in Classical Sanskrit Literature as well. The same is true in case of Modern Vernacular literature too.

1. *tabu bihaṅga, ore bihaṅga mor*
   ekhani andha bandha koro nā pākhā /
2. *aji kamala mukula dala khulila*
3. *dāktar phastār/iskul māster*
   bet tar cat pat/chātrera chat pat
   bhaye sab pastāy/bādi chede rāstāty

And lastly a poem composed in the late nineties can also be placed in the same catagory.

orā bhāble kellā phate
māl kaḍi sab nijer hāte
āmrā kajan māstuto bhāi
chū-mantar juḍi hākai |

Now we come to *Upacāravakratā*. *Upacāravakratā* is defined in *vakrokti-jīvita* by Kuntaka as yatra[22].......etc. wherein even when the two (*prastuta* and *aprastuta*) are far apart from each other, a common attribute is metaphorically superimposed and a fresh type of beauty is in the make and this type of superimposition of identity forms the basis of various pleasing and inventive figures of speech headed by metaphor – this is called *Upacāravakratā*. For instance:

1. *tat sūryasya devatvam tanmahitvam*
madhyā kartor vitatam samjabhāra
yadedayukta haritaḥ sadhasthā
dādrātri vāsastanute simasmai // – ṛgveda – 1/115/4

Herein the sentient qualities are metaphorically applied to non-sentient things.

2. *gacchantīnām ramaṇavasatim....*Kuntaka quotes from *Meghadūta*.

In this verse though darkness is abstract, in order to emphasize its immense density, the poet has metaphorically attributed the quality of being pierced by a needle which is really possible only in the case of a concrete object.

3. *bālenduvakrāṇi – Kumārasambham* III/29/
4. *bālasya lakṣmīn glapayantam indoḥ* – ibid II/49
5. *bāla-kadamba-kalpaih* – ibid III/68.
6. *bālānuṇavabhru valkalam* – ibid V/8
7. *bālamṛgākṣī mṛgyate* – ibid V/72
8. *bāla-mandāravṛkṣa* – Meghadutam /Uttaramegha/12

In all the above-mentioned cases '*bālatva*', a human attribute has metaphorically been imposed on the sun, the moon, the deer, the tree and on the creepers too.

Thus the variety of *Upacāravakratā* i.e. 'beauty in metaphorical expression' may be instanced in thousands and thousands in the tradition of good poets and may be gathered easily by us.

Due to paucity of time and space we have concentrated our discussion only within two varieties of *vakratā* – the former denotes the highest excellence in *śabdālaṃkāras* and the later denotes that in *arthālaṃkāras*.

Thus from the above discussion we may conclude whenever there is an urge for poetic or artistic expression there is no getting away from *vakrokti*, be it the ancient age of ṛgveda or the classical age of Bhāsa, Kālidāsa, and so on or even the modern era of 21st century. So no matter whether you support *Dhvani* school or *Rasa* school, *Alaṃkāra* school or Rīti school you have to admit that in all poetic expressions "*Saiṣā sarvaiva vakroktiḥ*».

Notes and References

1. Thomas Gray, Edmund D.Jones, ed. English Critical Essays (Sixteenth, Seventeenth and Eighteenth centuries), 1922. p-266
2. Foreword by R. K. Dasgupta, Vakrokti-jīvita – edt. by R. S. Bandyopadhy 1993 B.S., 1t ed.
3. Kāvyālaṃkāra of Rudrata – II/13 to 17
4. Sādṛśyāllakṣaṇā vakroktiḥ – kāvyālaṃkāra – sūtra-vṛtti-V/3/8
5. Kāvayādarsa of Dandin, edt. by R. Mishra, Chowkhamba Vidyabhavan, Varanasi, 1984, 3rd ed.
6. John Mukarovsky, Standard language and poetic language', intr. Paul L.
   Garvin, A Prague School Reader of Aesthitcs, 1964, p 27
7. Naiṣadhacaritam – IX/50 (edt. by Narayan Ram Acharya, New Delhi, 1986)
8. II/8, Kāvyālaṃkāra of Bhamaha 2/85
9. vakraibhidheya-śabdoktiristā vācāmalaṃkṛtiḥ – Kāyalamkāra of Bhāmaha I/36
10. vācāṃ vakrārtha-śabdokti ralaṃkārāya kalpate ibid V/66
11. Vakrokti-jīvita of Kuntaka ed. K. Krisnamoorthy-p-20
12. Vakrokti-jīvita of Kuntaka ed. K. Krisnamoorthy-p-20
13. Vakrokti-jīvitam – I/7
14. Vakrokti-jīvita of Kuntaka ed. K. Krisnamoorthy-II/1
15. varṇaśabda...etc. ibid P-74
16. Vakrokti-jīvita ibid II/2
17. Upanishadic Śāntipātha
18. Raghuvamśam – XI/15

19. Kumārsaṃbhavam – VII/76
20. Śiśupālvadham
21. Gītagovindam
22. Vakrokti-jīvita of Kuntaka ed. by K. Krisnamoorthy II/13,14

Select Bibliography

(A) Primary Sources

(i) Conspectus of Editions of **Sanskrit Texts** : [To which references are made in the paper]

- Kāvyādarśa of Dandin, with two commentaries, edt. by M. Rangācārya, Madras, 1910
- Kāvyalaṃkāra of Rudrata with Namisādhu's Tippaṇī, edt. Kāvyamālā 2. 1909
- Kāvyāmimāṃsā of Rājaśekhara, edt. Gaekwad's Oriental Series, no. 1, 1916
- Kāvyalaṃkāra of Bhāmaha, with English Transalation and Notes, edt. by P.V. Naganatha Sāstri, Reprint, 1991 of second edition, 1970, Delhi.
- Naisadhīyacaritam – with Nārāyaṇa-tīkā, edt. by Narayan Ram Acharya, New Delhi, 1986 (Reprint)
- Sahitya-Darpanah, with Kusuma-pratimā Commentary Siddhāntavāgīsa, Calcutta, 4th edition, 1867 śaka.
- Vakrokti-jīvita of Kuntaka – edt. by K. Krishnamoorthy, Dharwar, 1977 1st edition
- Vakrokti-jīvita – edt. by R. S. Bandyopadhyay, 1393 B.S, Calcutta, 1st ed.
- Vakrokti-jīvita – edt. by S.K. De, Calcutta, 1961, 3rd edition

(B) Secondary Sources

(ii) Works in English :

- Acharya Sitanath – "Kuntaka on poetic blemishes" Anvīkṣā, vol. XVII (1996-1997)

- Bandyopadhyay, G S – "An Analysis of Kuntaka's Concept of Style", Journal of the Department of Sanskrit, Rabindra Bharati University, Vol. I, 1984

- De, Sushil Kumar – History of Sanskrit Poetics, Complete Revised Edition, Firma KLM, 1988 Reprint, Second Edition, 1960 Calcutta.

- Gonda,J. – Remarks on similes in Sanskrit Literature, Leiden, 1949

- Kane, P.V. – History of Sanskrit Poetics, Fourth Edition, Delhi, 1971; Reprint Delhi, 1987, 1994, 1998

(iii) Works in Bengali :

- Acharya, Sitanath, i) *"Vakrokti-tattver vivartan"* published in 'Prabandhamālikā'. Calcutta, 2005

  (ii) "Kuntaker Kāvyacinta", Jahṇavi, Special issue, 1404B.S (1997)

- Bhattacharyya, Bishnupada, "Prācīn Bhāratīya Alaṃkār Śāstrer Bhumikā, Calcutta, 1360 BS

- Bhattacharyya, Sadhan Kumar – *Aristotle-er Poetics O Sāhityatattva*, Calcutta, 3rd edition, 1375 BS

- Chattopadhyay, Rita – *"Saiṣā sarvaiva vokrokti : prācīn sāhitya theke arbācīn sāhitya"*, Lectures on Sanskrit Poetics, (vol. 1), edt. by S.N. Chakravorty, Rabindra Bharati University, Calcutta, 2001

- Das, Karuna Sindhu – *Kāvyajijñāsar Rūparekhā*, Calcutta, 2nd edition, 1999

- Das Gupta, Sudhir Kumar – Kavyāloka (Pratham Khanda), 5th edition, 1386B.S

[Note – This paper was published in *Anvīkṣā Journal,* Vol – XXXII, March 2011 (Jadavpur University), Page – 69]

7

Classicality in Sanskrit:
Tradition and Innovation

বক্তব্যের প্রারম্ভে ভণিতা অংশকে বাদ দিয়েই বক্তব্য শুরু করা হচ্ছে। অধ্যাপকমণ্ডলীর প্রতি যথাযোগ্য সম্মান এবং ছাত্রছাত্রীদের প্রতি ভালোবাসা জানিয়ে এই বক্তব্য শুরু করা হচ্ছে। এখানে আসার পর তিনটি কারণ অত্যন্ত ভালোলাগার কারণ হয়ে উঠেছে। প্রথমতঃ এই সেমিনারের নির্বাচিত বিষয়টি অত্যন্ত প্রাসঙ্গিক, দ্বিতীয়তঃ এই বিষয় সম্বন্ধে আমাদের একটি ভ্রান্ত ধারণা রয়েছে যে "Classic" বলতে বোধহয় খুব পুরনো কিছুকে বোঝায়। এই বক্তব্যের মধ্যে এটাই দেখানো হবে যে আধুনিক সংস্কৃত সাহিত্যেও কীভাবে Classic/Classical/Classicality-র স্থান রয়েছে। তৃতীয়তঃ এখানে বিদ্যমান বক্তাদের মধ্যে আমি 'হংসমধ্যে বকো যথা', তথাপি আমি একমাত্র মহিলা। সেইজন্য খুব আনন্দ ও গর্বের সাথে বলছি। 'কুমারসম্ভব' – এ যখন পার্বতীর সাথে শিবের সম্বন্ধ হবে তখন সপ্তর্ষির সঙ্গে বসিষ্ঠপত্নী অরুন্ধতী এলেন এবং সমান সম্মান ও মর্যাদা পেলেন, সুতরাং এঁদের সঙ্গে একাসনে বসার সুযোগ পেয়ে আমিও আনন্দ অনুভব করছি। এজন্য প্রথম কৃতিত্ব অমিতবাবু, যিনি প্রথম আমাকে এখানে আসতে অনুরোধ করেছেন এবং দ্বিতীয় হল গোপা এবং দীপ্র, যারা অত্যন্ত সুন্দরভাবে আমাকে এখানে আসতে আমন্ত্রণ জানিয়েছে। এদের সকলকে ধন্যবাদ ও কৃতজ্ঞতা জানিয়ে শুরু করছি।

আধুনিক সংস্কৃত সাহিত্যে Classic/Classical/Classicality – র স্থান-

তিনটি point "classical" এর মধ্যে সবসময় থাকে-

i. তাকে খুব প্রাচীন একটা ভাষা হতে হবে, প্রাচীন থেকে যেটি এসেছে।

ii. অন্যকোনো Tradition-কে follow করবে না, যেমন – ল্যাটিন, গ্রীক ও সংস্কৃতের Tradition সম্পূর্ণ ভিন্ন।

iii. এর মধ্যে অনেক উদাহরণ থাকবে, কালিদাস, ভাস এঁদের লেখা সবই তার অন্তর্ভুক্ত।

তাহলে এখন যেগুলি লেখা হচ্ছে সেগুলিকে কী Classical বলা যাবে না? বিশ শতকের বাংলা সাহিত্যের ইতিহাসে যখন রচিত হবে তখন কিন্তু সুনীল গঙ্গোপাধ্যায়

এর এই সময়ে লেখা সবকিছুই classic বলেই পরিচিত হবে, তাকে এখন classic বলা হোক বা না হোক।

খুব সহজভাবে বলতে গেলে উদাহরণ দেওয়া যায় যে সঙ্গীতের ইতিহাসে মার্গ সঙ্গীত ছিল বা রাগপ্রধান গান ছিল, কিন্তু বিশ শতকে সলিল চৌধুরী সৃষ্টি করলেন "রানার ছুটেছে তাই ঝুমঝুম" – সঙ্গীতে ইতিহাস রচিত হলে কিন্তু এটা classic বলেই বিবেচিত হব। যা যুগে যুগে প্রচলিত থাকবে তাই "classic" এখন বিচার্য হল যে আধুনিক যুগে সংস্কৃত ভাষার রচিত সাহিত্যকে "Classic" বলা যাবে, না যাবে না। "Classical Literature" – ঠিক কাকে বলা হয় তা নিয়ে বড় বড় পণ্ডিতদের মধ্যেও মতভেদ বিদ্যমান। A.B. Keith, ম্যাকডোনেল, এ কৃষ্ণমাচারিয়া এ বিষয়ে তিনপ্রকার মত দিয়েছেন। একজনের মতে – "Classical Literature" হল বৈদিকসাহিত্যভিন্ন আর সবকিছু। অপর একজন বলেছেন – "Classical Literature" হল বৈদিক সাহিত্য, মহাকাব্য ও পুরাণ এই তিনটিকে বাদ দিয়ে আর সব। অপর একজন কিন্তু "Classic" এর মধ্যে Vedic, Poetry, Puranas, Dramma ইত্যাদি সবটিকেই গ্রহণ করেছেন। সুতরাং "Classical Sanskrit" বলতে কী বোঝায় তা নিয়ে পণ্ডিতরাও একমত নয়।

এখন আমরা কীভাবে Sanskrit Literature কোনগুলি তা বিচার করব? এই Classic কে কেউ বলেছেন উৎকৃষ্ট, কেউ বলেছেন অত্যুৎকৃষ্ট, কেউ বলেছেন ধ্রুপদী আবার কেউ বলেছেন উত্তমোত্তম কাব্য। কাব্য বলতে সংস্কৃতে দৃশ্য, শ্রব্য, গদ্য, পদ্য সবই বোঝায়, আর এগুলি যারা লিখেছেন তারা কবি। সংস্কৃতে কবি কথাটির অর্থ "Poet" নয়, কবি কথার অর্থ – "ক্রান্তদর্শী", যারা দূর/সবটা দেখতে পান। এবং এঁরা যখন কাব্য লিখছেন তখন তা অধিকাংশ ক্ষেত্রেই "Classic" হচ্ছে। যার জন্য আয়ুর্বেদ-এ ডাক্তারকে বলে কবিরাজ, কারণ "কবি" মানে "শ্রেষ্ঠ", তাদের জ্ঞানের পরিধি অসীম। তাই জন্যই তাদের "কবিরাজ" বলে। ভরত বললেন – "ন হি রসাদৃতে কশ্চিদর্থ প্রবর্ততে" – অর্থাৎ রস ছাড়া কিছু হতে পারে না। তাহলে কী যা রসপ্রধান তাকে বলা হবে "Classic"? আবার ভামহ বললেন – "ন কান্তমপি নির্ভূষং বিভাতি বনিতাননম্" – অলংকার ছাড়া কাব্যের প্রাণ আসে না। তাহলে কী যে কাব্যে অলংকার বেশী রয়েছে তাকে বলবো "Classic"? আনন্দবর্ধন বললেন – "কাব্যস্যাত্মা ধ্বনিরিতি" – কাব্যের আত্মা হল "ধ্বনি", "ধ্বনি" হল অন্তর্নিহিত অর্থ। তাহলে কী ধ্বনিবিশিষ্ট কাব্যই কেবলমাত্র "Classic"? কুন্তক বললেন – "বৈদগ্ধ্যভঙ্গীভণিতি" বা "বক্রোক্তি" – যা থাকতেই হবে, তা সমস্ত কাব্যের প্রাণ। যেমন – রবীন্দ্রনাথ এর রচনা, তাই তাঁর প্রতিটি রচনা "Classic"।

এ প্রসঙ্গে আচার্য গৌরীনাথ শাস্ত্রী রচিত "A Concise History of Classical Sanskrit Literature" গ্রন্থটির নাম উল্লেখ করা যেতে পারে। "Literature" বা "সাহিত্য" – কথাটি বিদ্যার সঙ্গে সমার্থক অনেক ক্ষেত্রে। সংস্কৃতে বলা হয়-

“অঙ্গানি বেদাশ্চত্বারো মীমাংসা ন্যায়বিস্তরঃ।
ধর্মশাস্ত্রং পুরাণঞ্চ বিদ্যা হ্যেতাশ্চতুর্দশঃ”

গৌরীনাথ শাস্ত্রী এই চতুর্দশবিদ্যাকে গ্রহণ করেছেন। কাব্য বলতে যেমন শ্রব্যকাব্য ও দৃশ্যকাব্যকে বোঝানো হয়েছে, তেমনই গদ্যকাব্যও তার মধ্যে অন্তর্ভুক্ত হয়ে পড়েছে। সংস্কৃত সাহিত্যে কবিতা, নাটক, ছোটগল্প সবকিছুই (কাব্যপদবাচ্য), এবং সেখানে সকলেই কবি। তাই নাট্যকার হওয়া সত্ত্বেও ভাসকে “মহাকবি” বলা হয়। “কবি” যাদের ব্যাপকতা অনেক গভীর।

প্রত্যেকটি ভাষায় “Classic” কথাটি ভিন্নভাবে ব্যবহৃত হয়। আমরা “Classical” বলতে বুঝি “Non-Vedic” – “Literature” কে। তাহলে কি বেদের মধ্যে Classical কিছুই নেই? নিশ্চয়ই আছে কারণ এই ভাগগুলি করেছেন পাশ্চাত্য গবেষকগণ।

এবারে “আধুনিক সংস্কৃত সাহিত্য” বা “Modern Sanskrit Literature” – আসা যাক। প্রথমেই হরিদাস সিদ্ধান্তবাগীশকৃত “মিবারপ্রতাপম্” নামক একটি নাটকের কথা বলা যেতে পারে, কেন প্রথমেই “নাটক” ? কারণ শাস্ত্রেই বলা হয়েছে – “সন্দর্ভেষু দশরূপকং শ্রেয়ঃ”। বিংশ শতাব্দীতে লেখা এই সাহিত্যগুলিকেও “Classic” বলা হচ্ছে। কারণ বিশ শতকে প্রাক্-স্বাধীনতা এবং স্বাধীনতোত্তর কালে রচিত এই নাটকগুলিতে নায়ক হয়েছেন কারা তা বিচার্য্য। এই সময়টির ঐতিহাসিক প্রেক্ষাপট খুবই গুরুত্বপূর্ণ। পরপর দুটি বিশ্বযুদ্ধ, স্বাধীনতা আন্দোলন, বঙ্গভঙ্গ আন্দোলন, ভারতের স্বাধীনতা প্রাপ্তি এবং তার পরবর্তী নানান রাজনৈতিক বিশৃঙ্খলা। এই প্রেক্ষাপটে নাট্যকাররা বেছে নিলেন কিছু নায়ক চরিত্র। যেমন-“শিবাজীচরিতম্”, “বাংলাদেশোদয়ম্” – শেখ মুজিবর রহমান এর নায়ক, “ধন্যোঽহং ধন্যোঽহং” – জি. বি. পলস্যুলে রচিত নাটক যার নায়ক সভরকর, ভগিনী নিবেদিতাকে নিয়ে রচিত নাটক “নিবেদিতনিবেদিতম্” – যার রচয়িত্রী ড. রমা চৌধুরী। ঝাঁসীর রাণী লক্ষ্মীবাঈকে নিয়ে রচিত “ভারতলক্ষ্মীনাটকম্”, রচয়িতা যতীন্দ্রবিমল চৌধুরী। এগুলি সবই “Classic” নাটক। আবার শ্রীজীব ন্যায়তীর্থ রচিত “মহাকবিঃ কালিদাসঃ” – নাটকটিও একটি Classic নাটক। কালিদাস “মেঘদূতম্” এ লিখলেন-

“তন্বী শ্যামা শিখরদশনা পক্কবিম্বাধরোষ্ঠী।
মধ্যে ক্ষামা চকিতহরিণীপ্রেক্ষণা নিম্ননাভিঃ।
শ্রোণীভারাদলসগমনা স্তোকনম্রা স্তনাভ্যাং
যা তত্র স্যাদ্যুবতিবিষয়ে সৃষ্টিরাদ্যেব ধাতুঃ।”

আবার শ্রীজীব ন্যায়তীর্থ লিখেছেন-

> "তন্বী শ্যামা রুচির-বদনা-স্নোজকান্তিং দধানা
> মধ্যে ক্ষামা নয়ন-কমলোন্নেয়-কর্ণাবতাংসা
> কম্বৌ বাহুবিটপললিতৌ বিভ্রতী শুভ্রদন্ত-
> জ্যোৎস্নাম্নাতাধরপুটদলা সৈব কান্তা মদীয়া।।"

দুটিই মন্দাক্রান্তা। কী অপূর্ব আনুগত্য কালিদাসের প্রতি। কালিদাসের হাতে মন্দাক্রান্তা, ভালো সহিসের হাতে আফগান ঘোড়ার তুল্য।

আর একজন Classic লেখক হলেন – মহামহোপাধ্যায় কালীপদ তর্কাচার্য। বিপুল তাঁর কবিপ্রতিভা। চণ্ডী এবং গীতার অনুবাদ করেছেন অসাধারণ। সেখানে গদ্যছন্দের অপূর্ব ব্যবহার করেছেন তিনি। জি. বি. পলস্যুলে যেমন সাভারকরকে নিয়ে নাটক লিখেছেন তেমনই মহাকাব্যও লিখেছেন – "বৈনায়কম্" – যেহেতু তাঁর পুরো নাম বিনায়ক দামোদর সাভারকর। এর সাথে আরও একটি "Classic" রচনার কথা বলা যায় মহামহোপাধ্যায় চন্দ্রকান্ত রচিত "চন্দ্রবংশীয়ম্"। এগুলি অবশ্যই অত্যুৎকৃষ্ট সাহিত্য বা "Classical Literature" বলে স্থান পাবে। প্রসঙ্গক্রমে বলা যায় রমা চৌধুরী তাঁর "নিবেদিতনিবেদিতম্" – নাটকে নিবেদিতার বিবেকানন্দকে প্রথম দর্শনের যে অনুভূতি ফুটিয়ে তুলেছেন, তা অতুলনীয়, নিবেদিতা বলেছেন – "কঃ এষ? কঃ এষ? কঃ এষ?" – অর্থাৎ ইনি কে? ইনি কে? ইনি কে? এই যে অনুভূতিকে নাটকীয়ভাবে ফুটিয়ে তোলা, এটিই নাটকটিকে "Classic" করে তুলেছে। মহাকাব্য তখনই সার্থক হয় যখন তার মধ্যে নাটকীয়ত্ব থাকে, যা কালিদাসের ছত্রে ছত্রে।

বিশ শতকে বাংলা ভাষায় "মেঘদূত" রচনা করেছেন যাদবপুর বিশ্ববিদ্যালয়ের অধ্যাপিকা দেবার্চনা সরকার। তার অংশবিশেষ হল-

> "কবে কোন্ কালে অবন্তীদেশে বিক্রমাঙ্ক রাজা
> কাজে গাফিলতি মনে করে ক্ষেপে কালাদাসে দিল সাজা।
> রাজার শহরে রয়ে গেল প্রিয়া, কালিদাস গেল চলে,
> এক বছরের শান্তি কাটাতে দূর পাহাড়ের কোলে।
> রামগিরি নামে সেই পর্বত, শোভা তার সুন্দর,
> সেইখানে এক আশ্রমমাঝে বানালো প্রবাস ঘর।
> কালকেটে যায় বর্ষা ঋতুর আগমনে ওঠে বেড়ে।
> আকাশের মেঘ বিরহীর মনে নেমে এল কথা টেনে।
> দূত বলে তাকে বরণ করলো নির্বাক (?) উন্মাদ।
> বার্তা পাঠালো জানাতে প্রিয়ার মঙ্গলসংবাদ"

-কালিদাসকে যক্ষের সাথে একাত্ম করে তোলা হচ্ছে, সেই সঙ্গে ধরা পড়ছে কালিদাসের প্রকৃতিচেতনাও। এটি কিন্তু অবশ্যই "Classic"।

তাহলে কোনটি "Classic" আর কোনটি নয়, তা কে বিচার করবেন। তার সমাধান সংস্কৃত শাস্ত্রকাররাই দিয়েছেন, তাঁদের মতে কাব্যের গুণগত মূল্যমান বিচার করবেন "সহৃদয়"। "সহৃদয়" কারা? তার লক্ষণ – "যেষাং কাব্যানুশীলনাভ্যাসবশাদ্‌ বিশদীভূতে মনোমুকুরে বর্ণনীয়তন্ময়ীভবনযোগ্যতা তে স্বহৃদয়সংবাদভাজঃ সহৃদয়ঃ" – এর অর্থ হল কাব্যানুশীলন ও অভ্যাসবশতঃ যার মন এত পরিষ্কার হয়ে গেছে যে তার মনোমুকুরে কবির বক্তব্য প্রতিবিম্বিত হচ্ছে তিনি সহৃদয়। অর্থাৎ ভাবয়িত্রী প্রতিভা প্রয়োজন। যার জন্য "নৈসর্গিকী প্রতিভা" বা "জন্মগত প্রতিভা", "শ্রুতং চ বহুনির্মলম্" বা নিষ্কলুষ জ্ঞান এবং "অমন্দশ্চাভিযোগঃ" অর্থাৎ একান্তসংযোগ প্রয়োজন।

রবীন্দ্রনাথ বলছেন – "কবিদের কী কাজ? সে আর কিছু না, আমাদের মনে সৌন্দর্যের উদ্রেক ঘটানো।" বঙ্কিমচন্দ্র এই সৌন্দর্যের সাথে যুক্ত করেছেন "চিত্তশুদ্ধীকরণ"। রবীন্দ্রনাথ বলেছেন – "কবিদিগকে আর কিছুই করিতে হইবে না, তাহারা কেবল সৌন্দর্য ফুটাইতে থাকুক। জগতের সর্বত্র যে সৌন্দর্য্য আছে তাহা তাহাদের হৃদয়ের আলোতে পরিস্ফুট, উজ্জ্বল হইয়া আমাদের চোখে পড়িতে থাকুক, তাহা হইলেই আমাদের প্রেম জাগিয়া উঠিবে, বিশ্বব্যাপী হইয়া উঠিবে।" – সর্বকালের সর্বকবির উদ্দেশ্য তাই। অবশেষে সমাপ্ত করা যাক হরিদাস সিদ্ধান্তবাগীশের একটি কবিতা দিয়ে-

"নবং নারিকেলম্ নবীনঞ্চ পেলম্

রমাঞ্চাপি নব্যাং গৃহং নূতনঞ্চ।

বচশ্চাপ্যপূর্ব্বং বিশেষেণ সর্ব্বে

রসজ্ঞাঃ পুরাণাঞ্চিরায়াদ্রিয়ন্তে।।"

-সুতরাং এই আলোচনার আলোকে উদ্ভাসিত নতুন তথ্য সহৃদয়ের রসতৃপ্তি বিধান করুক।

[*Note* – This paper was presented at the UGC Sponsored State Level Seminar on Depth of Classicality in Sanskrit, 2nd December, 2016, organized by Departments of History and Sanskrit, Gurudas College, in collaboration with Sanskrit College and University, Kolkata, and published by Gurudas College in the Seminar Proceedings in May 2018. This article appears on Pg - 29 of the published proceedings.]

আরণ্যষড়্বিংশিকা – একটি সমীক্ষা

কবি সীতানাথ আচার্য ও তাঁর কাব্য সম্বন্ধে আলোচনা করতে গেলে রবি কবির সেই পংক্তিটি বার বার মনে পড়ে-

'আমি পৃথিবীর কবি, যেথা তার যত ওঠে ধ্বনি
আমার বাঁশির সুরে সাড়া তার জাগিবে তখনি।'

সত্যিই আচার্য কবির 'দিবস বিভাবরী' ভরে উঠেছে 'সুরের গুরু'র অমূল্য, অবিশ্রান্ত এবং বিচিত্র দানে। সীতানাথের বাঁশীতে উঠেছে তাই নব নব তান, নতুন সুর, নতুন ছন্দ। 'সৃষ্টি সুখের উল্লাসে' মেতে উঠেছেন এই কবি বিচিত্র তাঁর কাব্যসম্ভার। কত কাব্যই না লিখেছেন সীতানাথ। সারস্বত চর্চায় যেহেতু সীতানাথ বৈচিত্র্যের সন্ধানী, তাই তাঁর কাব্য প্রবন্ধ সবকিছুই বিষয় বৈচিত্র্যে পূর্ণ। অন্যত্র বলেছি, 'বিভিন্ন ধরণের কবিতা বা কাব্য রচনা করেছেন আচার্য কবি, কখনও গীতিকাব্য – গীতিকাব্যের মধ্যে কখনও রোমান্টিকতাই প্রধান, কখনও বা সমাজের সমস্যা বা রাজনৈতিক বা আর্থ-সামাজিক সমস্যা রয়েছে কেন্দ্রবিন্দুতে, কবিতার মধ্যে কখনও মূর্ত হয়ে উঠেছে দেশাত্মবোধ, জাতীয়তাবোধ, কখনও রূপকল্পের মধ্যে ফুটে উঠেছে জটিল ঘূর্ণাবর্ত সময়ের প্রতিচ্ছবি, কখনও বা কাল চেতনায় আক্রান্ত পেলব কবিমনে ধূমায়িত বহ্নির প্রতিচ্ছবি, কখনও বা জগতকে দেখছেন ধ্যানীর মত গম্ভীরভাবে শান্তভঙ্গীতে, আর কখনও জীবনযন্ত্রণায় ক্ষতবিক্ষত মানুষের জন্য ডুকরে কেঁদে উঠেছেন।' (দ্রষ্টব্য – সীতানাথ আচার্য : কবি ও প্রাবন্ধিক, পৃঃ ১৫-১৬)

দেশের প্রতি, মাটির প্রতি, দেশমাতৃকার প্রতি তাঁর নাড়ীর টান একাধিক কবিতায় প্রতিধ্বনিত হয়েছে – কখনও অভিধার আশ্রয়ে, কখনও লক্ষণা আর কখনও বা সরাসরি অভিধামূল বা লক্ষণামূল ধ্বনির আশ্রয়ে।

একদিকে বর্তমানে পরিবেশ দূষণ অন্যদিকে ভারতীয় সংস্কৃতির মূল মন্ত্র পরিবেশরক্ষণ – পাশাপাশি তুলে ধরেছেন সীতানাথ তাঁর 'আরণ্যষড়্বিংশিকা' কবিতাটির মাধ্যমে। ২৬টি শ্লোকের সমন্বয়ে রচিত এই কাব্যে প্রধানতঃ অনুষ্টুপ্ ছন্দ ব্যবহৃত হলেও ইন্দ্রবজ্রা, উপেন্দ্রবজ্রা প্রভৃতি ছন্দের অনবদ্য প্রয়োগ কুশলতাও লক্ষণীয়।

অরণ্যদেবী অথবা অরণ্যমাতার কাছে মানবসভ্যতার ঋণ অপরিশোধ্য, চিরন্তন, অন্তহীন। মানবসমাজের শৈশব অতিবাহিত হয়েছে অরণ্যমাতার স্নেহসিক্ত কোলে। অরণ্যজননীর কোলে অবস্থিত সমাধিমগ্ন ঋতদ্রষ্টা ঋষিদের চিত্তে ঋক্‌মন্ত্র প্রতিভাত হয়েছে। সেখান থেকেই উত্থিত হয়েছে সামগীত।

'মাতঙ্গবাঙ্কে বসতাং শুভে পুরা
সমাধিমাস্থায় বিশোধিতাত্মনাম্।
বিচিত্রবর্ণাঃ প্রতিভাসিতা ঋচ-
শ্চিত্তে মুনীনামভবং চ দুর্লভাঃ।।'

'অরণ্য'-কে, প্রকৃতিকে এই যে মাতৃসম্বোধন, তাঁকে বার বার 'বরাভয়প্রদে' 'প্রদূষণবিঘাতিকে', 'শুভঙ্করি' ইত্যাদি নানা অর্থবহ বিশেষণে বিভূষিত করা – আমাদের মনে করিয়ে অথর্ববেদের ভূমিসূক্তের সেই মন্ত্র – 'মাতা ভূমিঃ পুত্রোহহং পৃথিব্যাঃ'। সেই মায়েরই অঙ্গচ্ছেদনে তৎপর আমরা। সীমাহীন আমাদের নিষ্ঠুরতা। আমাদের কি মনে পড়ে না – আমাদের অর্থাৎ এই মানবসভ্যতার বাল্য অতিবাহিত হয়েছে এই অরণ্য – মায়েরই কোলে-

'শৃণ্বতাং মধুরাং গীতিং
বিহগ কূজনাত্মিকাম্।
ব্যতীতং বাল্যমস্মাক-
মিতি ন স্মর্য্যতেঽধুনা।।'

অরণ্যের কোলেই আদিকাব্য রামায়ণ রচিত হয়েছে – 'ধ্বন্যালোক' কার বললেন-

'কাব্যস্যাত্মা স এবার্থ
স্তথা চাদিকবেঃ পুরা।
ক্রৌঞ্চদ্বন্দ্ববিয়োগোত্থঃ
শোকঃ শ্লোকত্বমাগতঃ।।'

তারপর থেকে কূলপ্লাবিনী কাব্যধারা সহস্রদিকে ছড়িয়ে পড়েছে।

'মাতঙ্গদীয়ায়তনে কদাচিৎ
স্নাতুং প্রযাতস্তমসাং স্রবন্তীম্।
মুনেশ্চ বল্মীকভবস্য চিত্তে
ছন্দো নবীনং সৃফুরিতং বভূব।।'

রঘুবংশের কবিও বললেন – ক্রন্দনরতা সীতার সামনে এসে দাঁড়ালেন সেই কবি কোন কবি? 'নিষাদবিদ্ধণ্ডজদর্শনোখঃ শ্লোকত্বমাপদ্যত যস্য শোকঃ' – ব্যাধের বাণে বিদ্ধ ক্রৌঞ্চকে দেখে যাঁর শোক শ্লোক হয়ে প্রকাশ পেয়েছিল সেই কবি।

কালিদাস, ভবভূতির কাব্যেও উপলব্ধ হয় অরণ্য প্রকৃতির শাশ্বত স্থান। অরণ্যদেবী, যে শকুন্তলাকে সযত্নে লালন করেছিলেন, তার পুত্র ভরতের নামেই চিহ্নিত হয়েছে আমাদের দেশ – ভারত। সীতানাথ কবি বলেছেন –

'অরণ্যলক্ষ্মি! ত্বয়কাতিযত্নতঃ
শকুন্তলা নাম সুতা সুপালিতা।
পুরা সুতং যা যমসূত সাধ্বী
তস্যাখ্যয়া নঃ প্রথতে হি দেশঃ।।'

প্রসঙ্গতঃ বলি, কালিদাসের কাব্যে এই অরণ্যপ্রকৃতি মানবসমাজের থেকে পৃথক, কোন সত্তা নয়, তাই তারা মানুষের সুখে হাসে, মানুষের দুঃখে কাঁদে। সীতার করুণ ক্রন্দন শুনে তাই ময়ূরের নাচ থেমে যায়, গাছের ফুল ঝরে পড়ে, হরিণীরা মুখ থেকে কুশের গ্রাস ফেলে দেয়। সীতার বেদনায় সমব্যথী অরণ্যও আকুল হয়ে কাঁদে-

'নৃত্যং ময়ূরাঃ কুসুমানি বৃক্ষা
দর্ভানুপাত্তান্ বিজহুর্হরিণ্যঃ।
তস্যাঃ প্রপন্নে সমদুঃখভাবম-
ত্যন্তমাসীদ্রুদিতং বনেऽপি।।'

তপোবনলালিতা শকুন্তলার বিরহে তপোবনের কান্না আজও আমরা শুনতে পাই। কুমারসম্ভবেও একই প্রকৃতিপ্রেম মূর্ত হয়ে উঠেছে।

আধুনিক কবি সীতানাথও ভোলেননি অরণ্যের আশ্রয়ে গড়ে ওঠা শান্তরসাস্পদ তপোবনগুলির কথা, ভোলেননি এই তপোবনগুলিই ভারতের বিশিষ্ট সংস্কৃতির উদ্ভবস্থল। অরণ্যের প্রেরণাতেই ঋষিচিত্তে উদ্গত হয়েছিল ঔপনিষদিক দর্শনচিন্তা। দূষিত বাতাস আত্মসাৎ করে নীলকণ্ঠ স্বরূপা অরণ্যমাতা আমাদের নিয়ত রক্ষা করেছেন। কিন্তু সেসব আমরা ভুলে গেছি –

'এতচ্চ সর্বং তব কর্মপূতং / প্রচ্যাবিতং ভাতি হৃদোऽদ্য মানবৈঃ।'

সীতানাথের প্রণাম যেন কবির ভাষায়-

'ও আমার দেশের মাটি
তোমার পরে ঠেকাই মাথা।'

ক্ষেমেন্দ্র তাঁর 'সুবৃত্ততিলক' গ্রন্থে বললেন – কাব্যে শৃঙ্গার, করুণ প্রভৃতি রসের অনুসারে এবং বর্ণ্য বিষয় অনুসারে ছন্দের প্রয়োগ করতে হবে। সীতানাথ তাই করেছেন। 'শিশুযুবদুর্দৈববিলসিতম্' কাব্যটির আলোচনা প্রসঙ্গে বলেছি, ক্ষেমেন্দ্র তাঁর সুবৃত্ততিলক গ্রন্থের দ্বিতীয় বিন্যাসে বলেছেন – 'তস্মাদব্যভিচারেণ শ্রব্যতৈব গরীয়সী'। অনুষ্টুপ্ ছন্দের লক্ষণ প্রসঙ্গে বলেছেন – 'অনুষ্টুপ্' এর ক্ষেত্রে অনেক ভেদ দেখা যায়। যে লক্ষণ করা হয়েছে তার অনেক ব্যতিক্রমও দেখা যায়, কিন্তু শ্রব্যতা অর্থাৎ শ্রুতিমাধুর্যই বিশেষভাবে বিবেচ্য। আগেই বলেছি, আবার বলছি সীতানাথের হাতে অনুষ্টুপ্ প্রয়োগের স্বচ্ছন্দতা, সাবলীলতার কথা। জানা বিষয়ের পুনরুক্তির অর্থ ছন্দঃপ্রয়োগে কবির বৈদগ্ধ্যের, মুন্সীয়ানার আত্যন্তিক গুরুত্বটুকু পাঠকের সামনে তুলে ধরা। আরণ্যষড়্বিংশিকা-র বিশেষ বিশেষ অংশে অনবদ্য অনুষ্টুপ্। তাছাড়াও এখানে ওখানে বন্দনাগাথা অথবা প্রশস্তিপত্র অথবা অভিনন্দন পত্রের ছত্রে ছত্রে রয়েছে সীতানাথের অনুষ্টুপ্। বারবার মনে হয়েছে – 'সুবশা সীতানাথস্য অনুষ্টুপ্ প্রবর্ত্ততি।'

ছোট্ট কবিতার মধ্য দিয়ে কবি সীতানাথের পাশাপাশি দার্শনিক ও বৈয়াকরণ সীতানাথও বারবার আত্মপ্রকাশ করেছেন। ৯নং শ্লোকে 'প্রয়াতঃ' শব্দটি 'মুনেঃ' এর বিশেষণ রূপে প্রযুক্ত। আপতঃদৃষ্টিতে মনে হয় 'ক্ত'-প্রত্যয়ান্ত শব্দ, কিন্তু প্রকৃতপক্ষে প্রয়াত শব্দের ষষ্ঠীর একবচনে নিষ্পন্ন – সেই মুনির চিত্তে 'স্ফুরিত' হয়েছিল। কোন মুনির – যিনি তমসার স্নানের উদ্দেশ্যে গমন করেছিলেন, যিনি 'বল্মীকভব'। 'নদী' অর্থে 'স্রবন্তী' পদের প্রয়োগও প্রশংসার দাবী রাখে। প্রাসঙ্গিক সেই শ্লোক-

'মাতন্তদীয়ায়তনে কদাচিৎ
স্নাতুং প্রযাতস্তমসাং স্রবন্তীম্।
মুনেশ্চ বল্মীকভবস্য চিত্তে
ছন্দো নবীনং স্ফুরিতংবভূব।।'

শব্দ প্রয়োগে আচার্য কবির মুন্সীয়ানা বার বার উপলব্ধ হয়েছে 'আরণ্যষড়্বিংশিকা' কবিতায়। সম্যক্ স্থিতি অর্থে 'সংস্থান' (১), 'প্রফুল্লত্ব' শব্দের ষষ্ঠীর একবচনে 'প্রফুল্লতাম্' (৪) ইত্যাদি প্রয়োগ বিশেষভাবে প্রণিধানযোগ্য।

যমক অনুপ্রাসের সব ভেদ – বৃত্ত্যনুপ্রাস, শ্রুত্যনুপ্রাস ইত্যাদির স্বচ্ছন্দ ও সাবলীল প্রয়োগ পাঠককে মুগ্ধ করে। 'পুরা সুতং সা যমসূত সাধ্বী' (১২), 'বিধীয়তাং বুদ্ধিবিশুদ্ধা' (২৫) '... চরিতঃ কিলৈতঃ' (২০) 'ক্লেশততিং ততান' (২০), 'বৃত্তিির্বিনিন্দিতা' (৩), 'কিঞ্চিৎ কদাপি কৃপয়া' (২১) ইত্যাদি অবশ্যই উল্লেখনীয়।

কবিতার শেষ দুটি শ্লোক কবি বিধাতার কাছে মানুষের শুভবুদ্ধির কামনা করছেন – মানুষ যেন আবার অরণ্যসৃজনে উদ্যোগী হয় – 'উচ্ছেদতোঽরণ্যভুবোঽচিরেণ নিবর্তিতাঃ স্যাম যথা চিরেণ', এবং 'স্বচ্ছন্দতঃ প্রতিগৃহং প্রতিভূমিভাগং সংরোপ্য বৃক্ষনিচয়ান্ পরিপালয়েম' (২৫, ২৬)। সেই শুভবুদ্ধির প্রেরণায় রবি কবির সুরে সুরে মিলিয়ে বলছেন – 'দাও ফিরে সে অরণ্য – লও এ নগর'।

রাজানক কুন্তকাচার্য এবং তাঁর বক্রোক্তিতত্ত্ব সীতানাথ আচার্যের সারস্বত সাধনার অন্বিষ্ট। সেই কুন্তকের ভাষায় বলি – 'ন কাব্যার্থবিরামোঽস্তি যদি স্যাৎ প্রতিভাগুণঃ।' প্রতিভা শক্তি যদি থাকে তবে কাব্যার্থের বিশ্রান্তি হয় না অর্থাৎ নানা প্রকার কাব্যার্থের নিয়ত সৃফুরণ ঘটে। সবশেষে এই প্রার্থনা, বিরল কবিপ্রতিভার আধার সীতানাথ কবির কলনাদিনী কাব্যধারা বয়ে চলুক স্বচ্ছতোয়া স্রোতস্বিনীর মত, অনাবিলা নির্ঝরিণীর মত।

[*Note* – This paper was presented at the UGC Sponsored State Level Seminar on Village and Forest Life in Sanskrit Literature, Department of Sanskrit, Bhatter College, Dantan, Paschim Medinipur, West Bengal, 6th April, 2009. This article was also published in the Seminar proceedings published thereafter by the Principal, Bhatter College, Dantan, Paschim Medinipur, on Pg 4.]

विगत-वर्ष-दशकस्य संस्कृत-नाटकानि (१९९०-१९९९)

विगतवर्षदशके विरचितानां नाटकानां संख्या तु भूयस्येव। वर्तमानगवेषिकया विगतवर्षदशके विरचितानि रूपकाणि त्रिसप्ततिसंख्यकानि संगृहीतानि, बहूनि पठितानि च। तेषां सर्वेषां केवलम् नामोल्लेखनमपि पत्रेऽस्मिन् न सम्भवेत् स्थानाभावात् कालाभावाच्च। तेषु केषाञ्चिद् दिग्दर्शनमत्र कृतम्।

आलोच्यनाटकानि तावत् मुख्यतः धाराद्वयमाश्रित्य वर्तन्ते।

1. पणप्रथाकुष्ठजातिभेदबाल्यविवाहादिकं समकालिकसामाजिकसमस्याजातमाश्रित्य विरचितं नवं वृत्तम्।
2. पुरातनम् रामायणाद्याश्रितम् स्वल्पज्ञातं बहुज्ञातं वा इतिवृत्तं नवीनदृष्ट्या नूतनाङ्गिकेन वा उपस्थापितम्। नाटकेषु कुत्रचित् गभीरः स्वरः ध्वनितः, कुत्रचित् व्यङ्गात्मको हास्यरसः (satire) परिवेषितः, क्वचिन्नाट्यकृतः आशा प्रतिफलिता, क्वचिन्निराशा हताशा वा।

पूर्वम् संक्षेपिकायाम् पञ्चदशरूपकाणि आलोचयितव्यानि इति उक्तमासीत्। तत्तु न सम्भवति। पत्रेऽस्मिन् वरविक्रयम्, बालविधवा, साक्षात्कारः, सोमप्रभम्, विडम्बना, एकचक्रम् इत्यादीनि कानिचित् रूपकाणि आलोचितानि कानिचित् प्रथमविभागतः कानिचित् द्वितीयविभागतः निर्वाचितानि किञ्च यानि सर्वाण्येव वस्तुदृष्ट्या वर्तमानसमाजस्थितौ सातिशयं प्रासङ्गिकतामवगाहन्ते।

अत्र नाटकम् इति शब्दः आङ्गलभाषास्थित 'drama' इत्यस्य बङ्गभाषास्थनाटकम् इत्यस्य, संस्कृतभाषायाः 'रूपकम्' इत्यस्य च समर्थकः।

अनूप:

(लीलानाटकचक्रम्, व्याङ्गालोर, 1993) कर्णटकस्य लीला राओ दयालु महोदयाकृतं दृश्यत्रयसमन्वितम् नाटकम्।

नाटकेऽस्मिन् नायकः अनूपः वयसि युवा, कुष्ठरोगग्रस्तः सन् परिवारं परित्यजति। कुष्ठरोगिणां कृते यदारोग्यनिकेतनम् लोकावयात् बहिरेव वर्तते तदेवाश्रयति, नास्ति तस्य गत्यन्तरम्।

अतः यद्यपि "कुष्ठरोगः न खलु संक्रामको व्याधिरेव अतः तस्मान् भेत्तव्यम्", "कुष्ठरोगाक्रान्ताः सर्वेष्वेव कर्मसु अधिकारिणः, न कथमपि ते परिवारात् समाजाद्वा वहिष्कारमर्हन्ति" इत्याकारानि विज्ञापनानि पुनःपुनरेव वेतारदूरदर्शनसंवादपत्रादिप्रचारमाध्यमैः, प्रचारमापद्यन्ते तथापि यत् कुष्ठव्याधिग्रस्ताः समाजात्

वहिष्कृता एव स्वपरिवारेषु अपि तेषाम् स्थानं नास्ति इत्येव नाटकेनानेन सुष्ठुतया प्रतिपादितम् इत्यतः वर्तमानसमाजस्थितौ अस्य प्रासङ्गिकता अनस्वीकार्या एव।

वरविक्रयम् – (नवरूपकम्, लक्ष्मी, 1992)

सोमप्रभम – (प्रेक्षणसप्तकम्, निउ दिल्ली, 1997)

कुर्यात् सदा मङ्गलम् – (नवमालती, निउदिल्ली 1997)

वर्तमानसमाजे कन्यायाः पिता कथम् वरपक्षेण अधिकपणलाभार्थम् पीड्यते, कथं वा पणप्रथा अस्मद्समाजे दृढतया एव प्रोत्थिता तदेव चित्रितम् डॉ रामकृष्णमूर्त्तिमहोदयेन विरचिते 'वरविक्रयम्' इति नाटके, राधावल्लभत्रिपाठीमहोदयेन विरचिते 'सोमप्रभम्' इति नाटके , डॉ नोदनाथमिश्रमहोदयेन विरचिते 'कुर्यात् सदा मङ्गलम्' इति नाटके च। अन्यान्यपि सन्ति बहूनि नाटकानि यान्येव पणप्रथाया विरोधितामुद्घोषयन्ति। नाटकानीमानि विहार-आन्ध्रप्रदेश-मध्यप्रदेशादिविभिन्नप्रदेशेषु विरचितानि किन्तु तेषां वक्तव्यं न विभिन्नम्, परन्तु साधारणमेव। अन्यथा कथम् (Life term) शीर्षकः संवादः संवादपत्रे आगन्तुं शक्नोते? 'वरविक्रयम्' इति नाटके व्यङ्ग्यात्मकः हास्यरसः (Satire) परिवेशितः अपरतः 'सोमप्रभम्' इत्यत्र, 'कुर्यात् सदा मङ्गलम्' इत्यत्र च गभीरः स्वरः ध्वनितः। नाटकेऽस्मिन् पञ्चमवर्षीयायाः सोमप्रभायाः साक्ष्यम् निपीडिताम् विमलाम् रक्षयति न खलु वास्तवसमाजे।

कुर्यात् सदा मङ्गलम्

लोकनाथमिश्रमहोदयेन विरचितम् षड्दृश्यसमन्वितं करुणरसाश्रितं नाटकमिदम् यस्मिन्नेव नाटके विंशशताब्द्यामपि नारीणां करुणा दशा तावत् चित्रायिता। नायिका नीरजा खलु आविवाहात् पितुः भारसदृशी, विवाहात् परमेव श्वशुरकुले पणार्थम् नितरां निपीडिता न केवलं मानसिकं निपीडनम्, कायिकमपि च। अन्तिमे सा एव तपिस्विनी निहता।

भवन्तस्तावत् कृपया त्रि-चतुर-पञ्चम-षष्ठसंख्याङ्कितेषु संवादेषु दृष्टिपातं कुर्बन्तु, सर्वत्र एव नीरजा विद्यमाना कुत्रचित् सा 'याज्ञसेनी', कुत्रचित् सुस्मिता, कुत्रचित् प्रतिमा वा परन्तु सर्वत्र निपीडिता, अन्तिमे निहता-, यौतकमेव सर्वत्र एकमेवाद्वितीयम् कारणम्। पणप्रथा सर्वत्र निन्दिता, यौतकं वर्जनीयम्, पणग्रहणं वर्जनीयम् इति सर्वत्रोच्चैरुद्घोषितम्, विधाइन्द्वारा निषिद्धम्, तथापि इदमेव यौतकग्रहणं चलितम्, इदमेव चलति, इदन्तु चलिष्यति। एवम् उक्तञ्च "प्रथनं कन्यादानम्, पश्चात् कन्यादहनम्, पूर्व वधूवरणम्, पश्चात् वधूदहनम्" इति।

पण्डितराजीयम् (नाट्यसप्तकम्, निउदिल्ली, 1992)

रमाकान्तशुक्लमहोदयेन विरचितम् अनवद्यम् रेडिओ-नाटकम्। पण्डितराजः जगन्नाथः ब्राह्मणः सन् शाह्जाहानस्य पालिताम् तनयाम् लवङ्गीम् सादरम् उपयेमे। समाजनेतृवृन्दः हिन्दु-मुसलमानयोः वैवाहिकं सम्बन्धं न कथमपि स्वीकरोति। अतः लवङ्गीं प्रति तेषां निर्यातनम् निपीडनम् कुत्सिताकारम् प्राप्नोति, लवङ्ग्याः मरणात् नास्ति उपायान्तरम् समाजनेतृणां शान्तये।

पश्चिमवङ्गप्रदेशात् आगताः सर्वे विगत 1995 ख्रीस्ताब्दस्य संवादपत्रशिरोनामविषयम् अवश्यमेव स्मरिष्यन्ति, यत्र कलिकातास्थाया कस्याश्चित् महिलाध्यक्षायाः, अन्तिमसंस्कारः न कृतः यतः सा मुसलमानधर्मिणः कस्यचित् कविवरस्य सहधर्मिणी आसीत्। अतः नाट्यकृत् प्रतिष्ठापयति सहस्रवर्षात् प्रागेव यः कुसंस्कारः दृष्टः सोऽधुनापि सर्वथैव नापगतः नवीनतया समाजे प्रतिष्ठित एव। यथा तथा वा भवतु पश्चिमवङ्गसर्वेकारेभ्यः तदा प्रभृति नूतना विधिः निर्दिष्टा यत् उपरतस्य उपरताया वा दाहः भविष्यति उत समाधिः वा तदुपरि धर्मस्य अनुशासनं न चलिष्यति, मरणात् प्राक् येन यया वा यदभिलषितम् आसीत् तदेव भविष्यति।

साक्षात्कारः (नाट्यसप्तपदम्, निउदिल्ली, 1996)

अभिराजराजेन्द्रमिश्रविरचितो नाटकेऽस्मिन् सर्वत्र चयन (Selection) विषये यदेव प्रहसनम् प्रतिदिनम् वर्तमानसमाजे प्रचलति तदेव व्यङ्ग्यात्मककहास्यरसेन सम्यगेव उद्घाटितम्।

महाविद्यालयस्य कार्यालयलिपिकस्य चयनं भविष्यति। M.A. उत्तीर्णः हिन्द्याङ्गलटङ्कणाभिज्ञः योग्यतमः प्रत्याशी परन्तु लिपिकपदे तस्य चयनं न भवति, भवति तु कृपालोः यस्य पुटकात् पत्रमेव निःसृतम्, पत्रं तु लिखितं राज्यस्य ऊच्चशिक्षामन्त्रीमहोदयेन। अतः अनन्तरामः उक्तः प्राचार्येण चयनसमितिमुख्येनयोग्यतातिशय्यात् स एव न मनोनीतः। "विशदीभूता तव योग्यता। त्वत्सदृशोच्चयोग्यतावन्तं जनं कथमहं लिपिकपदे नियोक्तुं शक्नोमि?"

विदुलापुत्रीयम् (मुम्बई, 1996)

एइच् भि. नागराजरावेण विरचितम् नाटकमिदं महाभारतस्य उद्योगपर्वस्थम् विदुलोपाख्यानमाश्रित्य विरचितम्।

इदं दर्शयति यत् समाजस्य शत्रवः न सर्वत्र बहिरागताः, परन्तु व्याधि-दारिद्र्य-दुर्नीति-प्रभृतयः अस्माकम् शत्रवः, अतः एषाम् विनाशाय सर्वथैव प्रयत्नः कार्यः।

एकचक्रम् (व्याङ्ग्गालोर, 1990)

विदुषा एन् रङ्ग्गनाथशर्मणाविरचितम् चतुरङ्ककविशिष्टम् लघुरूपमिदं महाभारतस्य आदिपर्वस्थितम् भीम-वकासुरोपख्यानमाश्रित्य विरचितम्।

वर्तमानसमाजे राजनैतिकनेतृणाम् नैतिक-अवक्षय-स्वार्थपरत्व-लोभादिकं प्रकटयतीदं रूपकम्। एकचक्रनगरस्य मन्दधीः दुर्बलश्च राजा, येन प्रतिश्रुतम् राक्षससकाशे – "प्रतिदिनम् आहारं वृषभादिमानुषञ्चेकं प्रेषयिष्यामि" इति। अथ राजा प्रजाः न रक्षति, परन्तु तेषां जीवनेन आत्मानं रक्षत्येव। एकत्र स्वार्थपरः राजा अन्यत्र ब्राह्मणपरिवारः यत्र सर्व एव प्रथमम् वकासुरस्य भक्ष्यो भवितुमुद्यतः। अस्ति च कुन्ती या 'सन्ति मे पञ्च पुत्राः, तेष्वन्यतमं त्वदर्थे प्रेषयिष्यामि' इति वक्तुं शक्नोति। अतोऽत्र रूपके महाभारतोपाख्याने नूतनत्वमापन्नम् इदन्तु स्वार्थपरत्व-परार्थपरत्वयोः चरमसीमानं प्रदर्शयति।

एतावत् पर्यन्तम् वस्तुदृष्ट्या नवीनत्वम् आलोचितम्। अधुना एतत् वक्तव्यम् यत् आधुनिकनाटकेषु संस्कृतभाषापि काञ्चिन्नवीनाकृतिमापन्ना यतः नूतनशब्दाः निर्मिताः, बाङ्ग्ला-ओडिया-हिन्दीप्रभृतिभाषाणां शब्दाः, अभिव्यक्तयः (Idioms) लोकोक्तयः अनायासेनैव प्रयुक्ताः, समकालिकभारतीयसाहित्यस्य वैदेशिकसाहित्यस्य प्रभावोऽपि अनस्वीकार्य एव।

उदाहरणानि परिवेषितानि बोधसौकर्याय, सनातनी प्राकृतभाषा वर्जिता, बङ्गभाषा, महाराष्ट्रप्रादेशिकभाषा, वैदेशिकभाषा अपि प्रयुक्ता, 'जननी' नाटकस्य प्रस्तावना उदाहरणरूपेण प्रदत्ता।

अधुना प्रतीकनाट्यानि नभोनाट्यानि गीतिनाट्यानि रचितानि, नाटकानि प्रायशः एकाङ्कानि, कुत्रापि पात्रादयः न केवलम् मञ्चस्थाः परन्तु दर्शकवृन्दात् एव समागताः। नाटकेषु बेकटब्रष्ट प्रभृतीनां स्मरणं जायते। (उदाहरणम्) कुत्रचिद्धा पात्राणि श्रेणीविशेषस्य प्रतिनिधित्वम् कुर्वन्ति, अतः स्वरव्यञ्जनसंहत्या एव परिचिताः। यथा कः खः गः घः इति, (अथ किम्) कुत्रचित् प्रेता एव पात्राणि, (चिताग्निः साक्षिरूपो वर्तते)। कुत्रचित् रोगः एव प्रधानचरित्रम्, कुत्रचित् नान्दी अस्ति कुत्रचिद् वा नास्ति। किन्तु प्रचलितप्रथा नानुसृता, एवम् भरतवाक्येष्वपि प्रचलिता प्रथा सर्वथा न अनुसृता, संगीतम् प्रवर्तितम्, कुत्रचित् श्रमिकगानम्, गजलगानम्, कीर्त्तनगानम् वा प्रवर्त्तितम्। (Flash-Back) प्रथा अनुसृता नेपथ्यध्वनिः (Back-ground music) अपि सुप्रयुक्तः।

अतः विगतवर्षदशकस्य संस्कृतनाटकेषु तावत् प्राचीननवीनयोः अपरूपम् सहावस्थानम्, ऐतिह्याविष्कारयोः अनवद्यम् सम्मेलनं दृश्यते एव इत्यलम्।

[*Note* – This paper was published in *Sagarika Journal,* Department of Sanskrit, Dr. Harisingh Gour Vishwavidyalaya, Sagar, Madhya Pradesh (35/3-4), Page – 33]